The Gospel of Gnosis

According to Philip

Commentary by Tau David Deschambault

ISBN: 978-0-9979047-1-0

Published by Kora Press
www.KoraPress.com

Printed in the United States of America

**KORA
PRESS**

Dedication

This book is dedicated to all the people I have ever met who, while living either in or out of the body, I have had the sacred privilege to share in both the trials and treasures of being human.

CONTENTS

INTRODUCTION

*T*he *Gospel of Gnosis* is a fertile interpretation of the good news. Its writings take much of its wisdom and strength from the ancient written and oral traditions of early Christians.

This fresh text distills the mysterious beauty of our ancestors and refines it for today's pilgrim. The quest of the wayfarer has not changed, and by today's standards its importance is still vital and universal.

The *Gospel of Gnosis* builds on the revelations of the past. It recognizes that the struggles of the past have become the building blocks for both today's joys and tribulations. For who we are as humans is a mere extension of free will and evolution. The *Gospel of Gnosis* reveals that who we are today is what we have become as a collective and ancient people. The problems and joys of today exist because that is who we are at this present moment. How we choose to live our lives at any given moment becomes our shared history. The world is simply reflecting back to us who we are and what we have created. As we learn to see more clearly through the eyes of *Gnosis*, we will discover that we are destined to be more than what the world currently reflects. If we live a life of contempt and evil, the world will only be able to reflect back to us contempt and evil. However, as we progress through the levels of *Gnosis*, what the world will reflect back to us is compassion and love.

The traditional myth of creation only speaks of one tree of life found in Paradise. This, of course, is the tree of knowledge which Adam and Eve ate from, which resulted in their minds being opened. However, we must also remember the mysterious allegory of the five trees which encompass our heavenly home, found in the *Gospel of Thomas*. Here Jesus said, "Blessed is he who was before he came into being. If you become disciples to me and listen to my words, these stones will minister to you. For you have five trees in Paradise which do not change, either in summer or in winter, and their leaves do not fall. He who knows them shall not taste of death."

In the *Gospel of Gnosis* we are guided through a conversation with the One. This is lovingly accomplished by the Holy Spirit's gift of contemplation and devotion to the human who seeks *Gnosis*. As with all growth, this happens in stages. For the wayfarer the five trees are the beginning of growth delivered in five steps of spiritual baptism, which originate from our true heavenly home. For the sojourner the mystical ascent begins in a trance, as it did for Adam and Eve. The *Gospel of Gnosis* reveals these baptismal states as first—enrobing, second—as washing, third—as enthroning, fourth—as glorifying, and fifth—as being caught up to luminous places.

The steps of baptism correspond with the stages of growth. The first stage of growth is beguilement, the second is defilement, the third is concentration, the fourth is discipline and the fifth is renewal.

As the burgeoning wayfarer passes through each stage of growth, they are introduced to five levels of internal angelic guidance. First is the catechumen (to ask), second is the neophyte (to join), third is the disciple (to begin), fourth is the noetic (to maintain) and fifth is the elder (to guide). After accepting their new virtuous identities the voyager is called forth to innately live the *Gospel of Gnosis* in the world. Once again the tree becomes the central motif of equanimity as depicted in the analogy of the tree with seven limbs. Finally, after faithfully living these spiritual realities, the sojourners are ready to depart this temporary world to receive the saintly reward and fullness of the beatific vision of Christ, where they continue to joyfully roam the eternal depths of Christ consciousness.

THE GOSPEL OF GNOSIS

THE GOSPEL OF GNOSIS

CHAPTER ONE

THE LIGHT OF THE ONE

*O*ur friend Thomas, the apostle of Yeshua, has shared with all the divine light of the One. There is an illumination emanating from within a person of light and it shines onto the whole world. We must seek the truth of heaven now and always. For the kingdom of heaven is with us always, but those occupied by the world do not see it. This yields ignorance of the One Holy Spirit. *(1.1)*

Thomas our brother has shared the words which the living Yeshua spoke. He has written them down for all of us to become stirred. Our Lord has said, "Blessed is he who came into being before he came into being. If you become my disciples, you will find five trees for you in Paradise which remain undisturbed summer and winter and whose leaves do not fall. Whoever becomes acquainted with them will not experience death." *(1.2)*

CHAPTER TWO

THE TEN HEAVENLY LAWS

*A*s for the time to come, Yeshua has given all who have ears to hear or eyes to see, the meekness of the way of heaven.

After gathering with those seeking peace, Yeshua taught in this way by saying, "Happiness comes to all by the reckoning of life and in the fulfillment of its mystery." *(2.1)* Yeshua then taught in a way which surpassed the old. He called forth all with ears to hear to be witness to the ten heavenly laws which bring wakefulness of the living Christ. *(2.2)*

1. Beware of the death of the body which is here and ever present.
2. Beware of how love drops to earth as a leaf in fall which no one can escape.
3. Beware of wealth as it wanes like the moon.
4. Beware of the world of distraction which embodies the spirit.
5. Beware of exhaustion which is the reward of wealth.
6. Beware of desire which weakens the spirit.
7. Beware of indulgence which casts confusion and doubt.
8. Beware of worldly concerns which consume vital spirit.
9. Beware of the outer search for truth.
10. Beware of the self which deceives and helps no one.

CHAPTER THREE

PARABLE OF THE INN

*T*he world is like an inn where you stay temporarily. None of the furniture is really yours. We will all be gone soon, for no one can stay long in an inn. Those who are self-serving do not take the resurrection seriously. *(3.1)* They are concerned with the surface and their spirit is depleted which causes them to rest before the time to rest has arrived. Their blindness leads them down paths of deception which causes the spirit to sleep, so when it awakens from its nightmare it is afraid and lost. *(3.2)*

CHAPTER FOUR

TWO PARABLES

Parable of the Mountain Grove

*T*here was a beautiful grove atop a mountain which cast a warm light on the forest below. Lovely and fragrant, it was said that it could satisfy any hunger or cure any illness. A sick and crippled man heard about this mountain, but could not make the journey because the road was long and the mountain high. He yearned to go but could never fulfill his dream. But as he became sicker, he felt desperate and reached out to a close friend who was both wise and capable. *(4.1)*

The friend made ladders and cut steps in the mountain where needed. By pushing and pulling, the sick man was able to make it to the summit where he was immediately healed. When the man felt the healing, he awakened to the love of Christ consciousness which had pulled and pushed him to the top of the mountain. *(4.2)* He then knew it was his faith which had healed him and not his presence atop the mountain. As he descended the mountain, he made an offering of his life's pain to the Creator for the common good. *(4.3)*

Parable of a Mountain Covered With a Forest

A follower asked Yeshua, "How can I be raised to eternal joy and peace?" Yeshua answered, "It is only nothing that can give rise to something. If it were any other way then peace and joy would never be. *(4.4)* Take, for example, a mountain covered with a forest. The leaves and branches of the trees spread shade everywhere. Surely, this mountain forest does not seek birds and animals, but they all come on their own to nest and gather. Or think of a great sea that draws all the rivers and springs and is vast without limits, and deep beyond measure. Surely, this ocean does not seek fish and scaly creatures. But they all dwell there on their own. Those of you who seek peace and joy are like these birds and fish. You need only soothe your minds and live quietly. Then in practicing these teachings you will not have to seek peace and joy, they will simply be there like the forest and the ocean. This is how nothing gives rise to something." *(4.5)*

CHAPTER FIVE

THE WAY OF PEACE

*T*he disciple then asked Yeshua, "How can I do nothing, but achieve everything?" Yeshua instructed the disciple to practice no desire, no action, no virtue, and no truth to follow the way of peace. *(5.1)* Again the disciple asked further of Yeshua, for he did not understand. Yeshua answered, "For the last time I say, your heart seeks one thing after another, creating a multitude of problems. You must not allow them to flare up. For doing things out of dreariness is not part of your true being. Cast aside vainness and shallow experiences. Do not try to find pleasure by puffing yourself up through good deeds. Practice instead kindness and charity for all. Do not be concerned with the facts, forget about right and wrong, sinking or rising, winning or losing. Be like a mirror, for it reflects all desire, action, virtue, and truth. This is the way to find the Christ. *(5.2)*

CHAPTER SIX

THE FIVE BAPTISMS

First Baptism: Release From Beguilement

*W*hen Adam and Eve ate from the tree of knowledge, they became enrobed, and rejected the power of the demiurge, and a sleep fell over their hearts and minds. However, each day of struggle slowly awakened them from a trance and the scales of seduction began to fall from their eyes. The light of day burned their eyes anew and the purification of mankind began and shall continue until the end of time. *(6.1)* A wolf in sheep's clothing was sent to devour the truth of mankind. Those who seek rest are seduced into an early sleep and are in peril of an eternal sleep that does not refresh. Those who awaken to the misery of such defilement are set on the path of righteousness. This is the first baptism of the catechumen, which releases him from the darkness of beguilement whose root is in the circle of trees which encompass Paradise. *(6.2)* From the beginning the spirit which now dwells in the psyche originated from the water of life. The first strand that enslaves is broken by this baptismal blessing. *(6.3)*

Second Baptism: Release From Defilement

*T*he Holy Spirit comes for the second time in the likeness of a female. Just as in the pangs of the parturient, the time for *Gnosis* approaches. *(6.4)* Those seduced begin to feel the burning of desire that leaves man needing more. Lost in the defilement of their own darkness, a glimmer of light faintly burns on the horizon. *(6.5)* With each motion towards the light, the light also moves toward a greater light. With each movement the light becomes brighter, but comes no closer until the appointed time. In the darkness the light shines on the face of evil and the Archigenetor is angered because its beauty is being lost. *(6.6)* This is the washing which awakens the neophyte to the future resurrection. *(6.7)*

Third Baptism: Release From Deception

*T*he third baptism awakens us to a sound that is foreign to us. We do not recognize it or know from whence it comes. It comes to put fear in our midst and mourning in our hearts. For now we shall mourn most bitterly. As for the future, let us make our flight before we are imprisoned once again and dragged into the bosom of the underworld. *(6.8)* For when we hear the voice which calls us forth, we follow it through the darkness and become enthroned and elevated to noetic heights. For the loosening of our bondage is upon us, and the times are cut short, and the days have shortened as our time is fulfilled. We grow from a tree which has its root in heaven. The tree which has no leaves and produced only the fruit of ignorance has its boughs broken by truth and the harvest of ignorance passes away. *(6.9)* When the disciple is given to the light of goodness, darkness fears the future. For behold, even as the Archigenetor hears for itself the sound of truth for the first time, it has no comprehending. It seeks the truth for itself but has no understanding of it and has no choice but to call forth all its depraved powers to crucify the disciple of the Lamb of God. *(6.10)* As the disciple is still weak, he must pray for the guidance of the Holy Spirit and trust in the One true light which calls him forth. *(6.11)*

Fourth Baptism: Release From Ignorance

*N*ow behold! All natures, all formed things, all creatures and their comforts, on their own and together, will be resolved into their own roots. This is why you become sick and die, because you love what deceives you. You become like the thing you love. Be careful that no one deceives you and may peace be within you. Be careful that no one leads you astray with, "Come over here," or "Go there." Follow only the child within. *(6.12)*

Those who seek peace will find it and will want to share it among their brethren. The child with the peace of Christ consciousness will be given access to the mysteries of the one voice revealed through the wisdom of Sophia. *(6.13)*

The voice of the perfect intellect will become the foundation for the All. What was once hidden will be glorified within them. For the One is both mother and father and copulates with itself. Therefore, it is not authentic to not know yourself. Examine yourself that you may know yourself, that you may understand who you are, in what way you exist and how you will come to be. For it is not fitting that you remain ignorant of yourself. For they who have not known themselves have known nothing, but those who come to know themselves have at the same time already achieved knowledge about the depth of the One. *(6.14)* Every noetic seeking and longing will find what they are looking for. And the eternal Holy Spirit will soothe, protect and love your essence back to fulfillment within the One true androgynous God. These are the glories which await the faithful who cast aside the garment of ignorance, for where the *nous* is, there rests all the beauty of Paradise. *(6.15)*

Fifth Baptism: Release From Consumption

S tripped of the garments of ignorance and clothed in the light which casts no shadow nothing will appear that belongs to the powers of the Archons. The time arrives when darkness will dissolve and ignorance will die. The bondage of the lesser has no sight in the presence of brilliance. However, a barb remains until the resurrection to remind us of the realm of giants. *(6.16)*

As they prepare to meet in the fullness of the eternal kingdom all brethren will gather and proclaim the ineffable through the power of the Holy Spirit with the renewal of Christ consciousness. *(6.17)* Tutelary renewal remains inexpressible to every sovereignty and every ruling power, except to the children of the light. The sovereigns who resign to the greater good truly learn to love their neighbors as themselves and leave a great gift upon the altar of peace. *(6.18)* Our teacher, Yeshua, instructs those who wish to find the treasure of paradise within to approach the altar of peace by passing through the gate along the narrow path of Christhood. The one who knows is called forth to serve the Prince of Peace, first as a disciple, and then as an elder who knows the will of the One and prepares to enter through the gates of Paradise. The elder who prepares for the resurrection rejects the power of kingship and embraces the authority of the Prince of Peace. *(6.19)*

CHAPTER SEVEN

The Resurrection of Truth

*S*ome people want to become learned. That is their purpose when they begin to solve unsolved problems. If they succeed, they are proud. But they have not stood in the word of truth. Rather, they seek their own rest, which we receive from our savior and our lord, the Christ. We receive rest when we come to know the truth and rest within it. *(7.1)* What, therefore, is the truth about the resurrection? For many do not believe in it, and few find it. So how does the One open the eyes of those who wish to come to know the resurrection? *(7.2)*

The Vision of the Blind Servant

A man went before his master for stealing a loaf of bread to feed his family. When asked by his master whether he was guilty of stealing the loaf, the man said no. When asked if he denied taking the loaf, the man said he had indeed taken the loaf. Since the man had no defense but his own, he was asked to give a good reason for his actions. The man stated that taking the loaf was not a theft because he took it out of his need and not his want. He then accused his master of neglecting his workers while he and his family would eat to excess. To this the master replied in judgement that as we are seen in this world, so do we clothe ourselves. He then sentenced the man to death and his family to labor. *(7.3)*

The Swallowing of Death

*W*hen the man faced his executioner, he was given a vision of how he had been seen in this world. He saw his flesh worn like an old garment that had become torn and worn out. For how we are seen in this world we wear like a garment. *(7.4)* Then the savior revealed to him the sunset of his life and held him in his arms as he was drawn into the One by beams of radiant light. Then, as the executioner's hand fell, he was drawn to heaven by the sun, on what appeared to be beams of light and nothing could hold him down. All that remained was his garment. This is the resurrection of the spirit, which swallows up the flesh. So as the world is clothed, so will it be judged. *(7.5)*

The Superior Way

*I*n the beginning a course may be followed that espouses a slight deviation with every advancement that continuously provides greater room for error. Our concern is not to be sinless, but to be one with God. *(7.6)* Thus the self-knower is a double person. *(7.7)* There is the part which he understands by rules and standards within itself. However, there is also the other part and its understanding has become something new throughout. It has struggled to become a superior being. *(7.8)* This latter part knows itself as no longer man, but at one with the Divine Mind. This is the spirit in motion, as it passes from one act to another. *(7.9)* The lesser part must work towards the evolution of its being. Only thus can it reproduce the higher. Something exists within which is higher than the self. *(7.10)* Eternity calls forth life to repose, complete itself, and become endless. For within itself many things are engraved to be held by the eternal engraver. *(7.11)* There is no injustice when a man suffers due to the condition he finds himself in. We cannot ask to be happy when our actions have not earned us happiness. The good are happy because they are good. For happiness is only found in living the virtuous life. When the seekers discover virtues' divine purpose, they will be raised above the crowds. *(7.12)*

The Real and Visible Resurrection of Life

*T*he visible parts of the body will not rise. Only the living parts which exist inside will rise. Therefore, what is the resurrection? *(7.12)* It is the revelation of those who have risen. Do not suppose that the resurrection is an illusion. It is no illusion. It is the truth. It is more proper to say the world is an illusion, rather than the resurrection of the Christ. *(7.13)* Do not become lost in the words of false prophets or lose yourself in details regarding the resurrection. Live according to the truth which does not obey the flesh for the sake of harmony. Flee from all deceitfulness which can be seen gathering like a coming storm. For truth cannot hide itself and will free your being from the bondage of false witnesses. *(7.14)* There are many ways for those who are still searching to find the truth that lead to eternal life through the One Christ. Do not roam aimlessly in error, only at the end to recover what one was at the beginning. Be released from the elements by these words which have been given to all by the generosity of the Creator. *(7.15)*

CHAPTER EIGHT

The Parable of a Slave

*Y*eshua said, "All have the ability to awaken, yet do not know it. Many prefer to drift on a great sea chained to an oar and suffer a lifetime as a slave. You are ignorant of what you possess and are chained to the oar which has been set below." *(8.1)*

The Tree With Seven Limbs

*Y*eshua spoke, "Each season, a tree with seven large limbs grows. It becomes stronger and sends out new shoots. It is not something that happens once and is complete. It is growing all the time. So it must be with you." *(8.2)*

The first limb offers repose from the heat of the day. If we sit long enough in its shade, we will remember. When we begin to remember, we will never forget our root and the relationship with what has been lost will continue, as we rise to our feet and climb. *(8.3)*

The second limb will reveal the leaves which return to the earth and become part of our future. As the buds of the tree reveal themselves, minds are raised to the questions of life. *(8.4)*

The third limb produces the fruit of faith, which encourages stamina and endurance to continue the ascent. *(8.5)*

The fourth limb produces the fruit of spiritual ease and restfulness, which is awakened from the worries of the world. *(8.6)*

The fifth limb produces the fruit of ecstasy with a view of the beauty beyond the hills, where joy and happiness await. *(8.7)*

The sixth limb finds stillness from the rustling of leaves where the voice of *Gnosis* can be heard. *(8.8)*

The seventh limb produces the fruit of wisdom where one rests in the arms of true love. *(8.9)*

CHAPTER NINE

THE DESTINY OF HUMANS

*Y*eshua was again questioned by the one who loved him most, who asked, "Will all souls be led into the pure light?" The Master then replied, "These are great matters that have risen in your mind and are difficult to explain to anyone except those of the unshakable race." *(9.1)* "Those upon whom the Holy Spirit of the living will descend and whom the spirit will empower will be saved and become perfect and worthy of greatness and be cleansed of all evil and the anxieties of wickedness. For those who refuse to embrace an anxious world worry not for the incorruptible and must concern themselves from this moment on without anger, jealousy, envy, desire, or greed for anything." *(9.2)* It is therefore not as Moses spoke. Adam did not fall into a sleep, but rather this trance-like state was a loss of sense. Thus the mind becomes sluggish that it may not understand or discern. *(9.3)*

Before the washing of feet the Master lastly received one more question from the one who loved him. "Where will the souls go when they leave their flesh?" With this the Master laughed and said, "The soul in which there is more power than the contemptible spirit is strong." *(9.4)* "She escapes from evil and through the intervention of the incorruptible one she is saved and taken up to eternal rest." *(9.5)* "Those who do not belong to the unshakable race will swim in forgetfulness. They will not awaken until they are once again thrown into the flesh. I have now told you everything to communicate secretly to your spiritual friends. These are the mysteries of the unshakable race." *(9.6)*

CHAPTER TEN

PEACE BE WITH YOU

*T*hose in the presence of Yeshua came to know him and love him. When reclining at table with his followers for the last time, he taught in this way, "If there is anything among my words that forms a dark cloud on the horizon, do not be worried about consulting the Christ within, who is always with you. *(10.1)* Whoever loves you will love your family. Anyone in this circle embraced by the Christ can help. However, beware of those who come to devour in my name. Always put goodness as well as evil to the trial as a test for the Holy Spirit. *(10.2)* For the resurrection is here now and always. *(10.3)* Remember, those who are only beginning will think differently about these things. Trust in your journey, as they must trust in theirs. Follow your light given to you by the Holy Spirit and do not pay attention to the designs of the day. *(10.4)* For those who die sober, as well as those who die drunk, will face the same God. For as the world is clothed, so will it be judged. May this be the measure of peace, so the grace of Christ may be with you always." *(10.5)*

CHAPTER ELEVEN

THE HAND OF THE CREATOR

*W*hen you break bread, do so not in my memory, but rather to remember what I came to teach the world. *(11.1)* The Creator's hand is on the chosen. Therefore strive first to be good and all else will follow. Go to the places where goodness lives. Then go to those other places and goodness will follow. This is the path which I have laid before the world, and now is the time to awaken and follow me. *(11.2)*

Introduction to Commentary

by Tau David Deschambault

*T*he *Gospel of Gnosis* encompasses a rare combination of ancient and contemporary insight. It is an example of the diversity of spirit which the spiritual seeker must open their minds to as they follow their hearts home. On the path the seeker will meet many other travelers. From the old literal world to the new natural world—these movements of the heart are discerned as the *Gospel of Gnosis* is paired with the old and new religions. Where east and west meet, both gospel and sutra become one within the Divine mind of God.

The *Gospel of Gnosis* has laid before us a spiritual map to discern and navigate the old world order, an order which is being consumed by the fire of systemic burnout. What will the fire leave in its place? What new order is preparing to rise anew from the ashes of the old? To answer these questions the *Gospel of Gnosis* has been synthesized into five parts.

In spiritual numerology the number five is the most dynamic and energetic of all the single-digit numbers. It is unpredictable, always in motion and constantly in need of change. Although it is molded from an almost equal mix of masculine and feminine qualities, in general the number five is slightly more feminine. It is extremely independent when influencing the mind and soul. The number five is uncompromising in its demand for freedom of thought and action. She makes up her own mind, rebels against any and all dogmas and ideologies, and does not allow herself to be absorbed into clubs, cults, religious sects or ideologies of any kind. The number five is therefore perfect to say goodbye to the old as she prepares to accept the new. She is the leader the world has been waiting for. The *Gospel of Gnosis* is the fifth gospel which is now ready to be accepted by the world. Let us now make a closer examination of the *Gospel of Gnosis* according to Philip and explore these five humanities of the human spirit.

At first glance the *Gospel of Gnosis* may seem to be fragmented. But after closer examination its true beauty can be found in its subtly flowing light of truth. The concept of five basic building blocks introduces the reader to the motif of unity through extra-legal representation. The five baptisms introduce the seeker to various stages of growth, which lead to deeper and deeper levels of angelic guidance. Everything begins with the seeker entering into each of the progressive five baptismal stages of growth. These stages are part of our shared human experience of growth as spiritual beings—spiritual beings who are destined to become one with the Divine. As we awaken we recognize our true spiritual identity as individual and collective thoughts of the One. We must seek strength to find the Divinity within ourselves. We have become undisciplined in the spiritual discernment of the inward and seduced by the ignorance of our material senses.

We begin this journey of materialization at birth. We put on the garment of the body as a single thought of God. As part of God, we have always been spiritualized, but as we face birthing into a body, we become part of matter. This new evolution of the spirit is a very difficult trial, but it is one worth taking. Those who say yes to this union of body, mind and spirit will grow in the ineffable mysteries of a loving universal life force. For those who choose the lesser challenge of denying spiritual realities may become imprisoned in the lesser and the immature false spirituality of materiality. This is why the world of seduction allures so many. The naïve spirit simply avoids the responsibilities of the soul. This is what gives birth to reincarnation, rather than the integration of the human spirit. For there is one essential truth, and four ways that this truth manifests in society, regardless of its transcultural expression. The truth is that there is no such thing as sin, only ignorance. And the four manifestations of ignorance are Enmity, Greed, Dissonance and Piety.

Ignorance

Ignorance is seen as lacking the ability to see truth in the light of wisdom. It is a type of sleep which leads to blindness. Put simply, this is the absence of *Gnosis*.

Enmity

Due to ignorance, enmity finds a home in the soul. Enmity's influence can be seen as racism, biases, animosity, hatred, and ill will.

Greed

Because ignorance has given enmity a home, greed now makes its move and acts like a predator of lost souls.

Dissonance

As greed prowls the depths of ignorance, all sense of dissonance is lost.

Piety

Finally, this lack of dissonance provides ignorance with the pious illusion that it has personally been called to do God's work on Earth.

At this point it is necessary to see how ignorance actually survives in the soul. So let us now discern the meaning of the five baptisms and all that follows by accepting the reasoned formula which the *Gospel of Gnosis* has so lovingly bequeathed to us. For the sake of ease, the headings for each baptism may be broken down into the following:

Beguiled Mysticism
Emotional Defilement
Noetic Concentration
Transcendent Discipline
Tutelary Renewal

Beguiled Mysticism

Beguiled Mysticism is a type of possession. So what does it mean to say someone is possessed? Have you ever seen someone possessed? What led you to believe they were possessed? Can you even recognize a possessed individual or culture? I ask these questions because many people walk the Earth possessed and do not even know it. For this reason possession has become difficult to recognize. People have become so entrenched in the material world of the senses they have lost the gift of wisdom. The mind along with its gift of wisdom has been lost to many. From this perspective we could discuss greed, lust, envy and many other human imperfections. But let us look at something more subtle—so subtle that it has become part of our everyday vernacular. This new vernacular uses words like depression and suicide. Both depression and suicide are epidemic in the so-called civilized world. I recently heard a man share the following story: *"As I sat in my dark hotel room I loaded the pistol and placed it into my mouth. I caulked it and thought about squeezing the trigger. At this instance I knew even in my pain and depression I was still a good person. I knew I did not want to die. All I wanted to do was kill the demon within me."*

This is a good example of what beguiled mysticism is. It hides in the darkness of popular culture and becomes normalized to the point where corporations and psychological gurus benefit from the pain of others. The soul has been skillfully separated from the herd so it can be singled out to feed the insatiable appetites of the ignorant.

The soul born into a body is merely passing through an evolution of spirit on its return to the source. This source is the home of the One Divine Mind. The intellectual principle of the human mind will have to overcome many trials before it finds ultimate peace as part of the Divine Mind. The deceptive demon of de-evolution can only survive within a host, for it has no insight to be able to look beyond the materialization of the senses. So it must seduce humanity for its sustenance; it must become the proverbial wolf in sheep's clothing and beguile the soul at every opportunity.

So how does this happen? Quite simply, the soul naturally seeks the spiritual, which manifests in the material world as mysticism. Therefore, the demon uses a false beguiled mysticism to entrap the soul in matter. A good example of beguiled mysticism is liquid mysticism. This is when the soul is seduced into believing that alcohol can provide the fulfillment which it is looking for. Just ask any recovering alcoholic what attracted them to alcohol in the first place, and they will say something like, *"Alcohol was my best friend who supported me no matter how difficult things became.''* Alcohol beguiles the soul, which is only following its natural desire to connect with the Divine Mind through mystic experience. When the soul is beguiled, it is taken down a path of destruction. However, once the alcoholic breaks free of the delusion called denial, his or her soul can return to its true path.

However, here we must be careful because the demon does not give up and this is when its tactics will change. It will try to seduce the soul by any other means at its disposal. In the world of addiction there are many lesser gods to follow, for addiction is simply another form of greed. Greed wants it now, and it wants all of it, and if it can't have it right now, it will steal it from someone else. Greed is deeply entrenched in the lower self and society at large, and is fueled by ignorance. As such, the lower soul, which innately wants to soar to its rightful place in the higher realm of the spiritual, is obstructed in doing so by the chains of a lower soul trapped in the material senses.

Beguiled mysticism is simply anything the demon within can use to gain a foothold so it can live within its host like a disease. In fact, beguiled mysticism is a disease of the soul and the only way to purge oneself of this disease is to find the strength to go within and do battle. For the demon is a coward and will not come into the light on its own. Once brought into the light, can a demon find peace within the mind of God? This is a question best left unanswered. To debate this only encourages engagement with the demon and the trap of beguiled mysticism is set up again. This question can only be answered by the Divine Mind of God in the fullness of time. So do not be seduced. Keep your mind focused on the finish line where our true God awaits our return from the material world. Our calling is to live our daily lives learning how to prepare for the death of the body and life thereafter.

Does it not make sense that before the material world existed, the Divine Mind was already present? Likewise, does it not therefore make sense that when the material world was created, each disembodied soul had to pass through the material world and experience an embodied human soul before its complete incarnation within the Divine Mind? In doing so it would have travelled full circle from the womb of the One, to birthing in the world, to returning to the One in fullness.

As people, we can say intellectually that we are all connected in body, mind, soul, spirit, earth, water, wind, and fire. But it is not enough to have an intellect. Robots have an intellect. But they do not have a soul. If we do not transcend the garment of the body, then the material world will become a trial for the soul through many lives.

The soul naturally seeks the mystical and, as it looks within through the gift of courage, it will begin to truly see itself in the mirrored face of God. Let us not be deceived by a beguiled mysticism. This is the beginning of the enrobing of the catechumen.

Emotional Defilement
The death we now speak of is the death of ignorance and selfishness through spiritual rebirth. This death is the birthing of love which is neither mortal nor immortal. For love is a Great Spirit. Love is the incarnation of the Divine Mind of the One. God is love and we are created in the image of love.

If beguiled mysticism is ignorance of love, then emotional defilement is the next progressive stage of sleep which needs to be overcome. As we awaken from beguilement, we are called to enlarge our horizon of understanding by opening our hearts to the love of the Divine Mind. However, to benefit from the many opportunities for personal growth, we must be able to see through layers of melancholy. For emotional defilement is not only a stage of enslavement; it can also be the next stage towards an awakened soul.

In this stage we begin to feel the pangs of conscience. We begin to further awaken. The purpose of emotional defilement is to keep the individual imprisoned within the body of emotions. We may experience anger, shame, remorse, resentment, guilt, or any other number of what we call negative emotions, which keep us captive. To break free from this captivity we must learn to put aside all the trappings of a beguiled spirit which is only interested in the shallow promises of the material world. Seduction by the world implies that we can accumulate enough power to acquire anything we want, including happiness. This is the grand seduction of greed which is an attempt to convince individuals and communities that by putting aside their emotional life they can rise to the status of a god. The innate desire to be one with the Divine Mind is now perverted as in beguiled mysticism to believe that emotions are for the weak minded. As a result, emotions are defiled and we compromise our souls by lying, cheating, stealing, and coveting all that belongs to another. Our emotions are trapped within us alongside the trappings of the material world. They intermingle, and as a result, the soul is forced to conform to the needs of emotional defilement. The soul will now crawl deeper into the corner of its prison cell. The only feeling it can muster is melancholy. This is the task of emotional defilement—to keep the soul depressed and indebted to its captors. This is what we have come to know as psychological or emotional reliance.

However, the soul will always hold onto something of its past. Therefore, while imprisoned, it will be forced to look deeply and will remember something of its past. It cannot give up and will always pray for the light of love. In this desire for love, emotional defilement begins to lose its power over the soul. The soul remembers something from before it had entered the body that still exists at its center. Its senses are now awakened to something more than beguilement. Its senses want something more than the emptiness of materialism. It now desires the human good, which now becomes possible. But emotional defilement is not ready to surrender and bombards the soul with false accusations and claims of iniquities. The battle within becomes alive with rumors, followed by emotional tests and trials. At times the soul may become tired and wants to return to the familiarity of the prison cell. However, as the battle continues, the demon cannot defend what is a lie and surrenders the ground it has captured to plan another strategy. But as the soul now ponders the view from higher ground, it can see the light anew and strives to overcome its emotional defilement.

This battle of emotion against emotion once again leads to conformity of spirit. But this time the emotions are lifted out of the mud of defilement and band together as one. The soul has tamed the negative emotions, and they become united within the person. The awareness of the interior life is maturing, and the emotions become a moral compass for the soul. Depression and melancholy are befriended by love actualized. The concept of the good appears and can be experienced. An interior marriage of male and female emotions gives life emotional congruency. With this balance the moral compass is steadied and the search for the human good continues. This is what we now understand as the washing of the neophyte.

Noetic Concentration
With the development of new awareness, the good can only be maintained with effort. As the soul begins to find itself, it now

experiences dissonance at its center. Its ego becomes enlarged and the demon now attempts to exert itself through ego attachments. The noetic world of beauty can be appreciated but not held. In public life the ego says one thing, but in private life it may say something completely different. Henceforth the dilemma of temptation is tested on the battlefield of dissonance.

The Divine Intellect becomes the reasoned principle in which the inner turmoil of dissonance can be resolved. With each battle fought there are winners and losers. Sometimes the soul wins, and other times the demons win. But with each experience we can continue to grow in self-awareness and wisdom, if we don't totally return to emotional defilement.

Through wisdom the concept of sin is now understood as a trap of the demon, which is just like its father, the devil. For both the concept of sin and the devil are human constructs of the mind fostered by the lower self, which is still being forged within the furnace of ignorance. Through noetic concentration and study, the process of personal growth begins to relieve the soul of superstitions. Free will now begins to take the advantage and the soul develops a mindfulness that guides the ego from dissonance toward detachment and liberty.

These trials are tests which become the ebb and flow of daily life. The individual now must learn to enter the abode of the underworld and develop the wisdom of seeing in the dark. This process requires stamina and can only endure within the church of the mind. The deeper this church is penetrated into, the closer we become one with the light within which casts no shadow. Ego attachments become fewer, as the soul becomes more detached from the seductions of the material world. The search for *Gnosis* now becomes the soul's priority, as it fosters meaning and aligns to its life's purpose.

Once we begin to awaken, noetic concentration not only shows us how high we can ascend, but also how low we can descend if we return to a sleep which is neglectful of our relationship with the One. At this point we have come a long way. However, the journey is not over yet and the demons who hunger to devour the soul know it. Vigilance, endurance, stamina, healthy friendships, and mentors are the staples for daily life, along with renewal rituals that awaken and enlighten. Here the soul experiences the enthroning of discipleship.

Transcendent Discipline
We all know how difficult it can be to live a disciplined life. To create change through will power alone is stressful. This is because willpower is a finite energy resource. There is only so much of it which can be directed to any given situation. Willpower on its own is a form of beguilement. It can be the same as saying, *"My will be done."* But transcendent discipline is something different. It is an infinite resource, if we learn how to use it. Transcendent discipline removes stress and worry. It is what is meant in the Lord's Prayer when we say *"Thy will be done."* Let's return to our alcoholic friend who may say it this way, *"We came to believe that a power greater than ourselves could restore us to sanity."* This is a type of surrender which is not giving up. It is giving oneself over to the One. The poem *Footprints in the Sand* illustrates what transcendent discipline can mean for some:

One night I dreamed a dream.
As I was walking along the beach with my Lord.
Across the dark sky flashed scenes from my life.
For each scene, I noticed two sets of footprints in the sand,
One belonging to me and one to my Lord.

After the last scene of my life flashed before me,
I looked back at the footprints in the sand.
I noticed that at many times along the path of my life,
especially at the very lowest and saddest times,
there was only one set of footprints.

This really troubled me, so I asked the Lord about it.
"Lord, you said once I decided to follow you,
You'd walk with me all the way.
But I noticed that during the saddest
and most troublesome times of my life,
there was only one set of footprints.
I don't understand why, when I needed You the most,
You would leave me."

He whispered, "My precious child, I love you and will never leave you
Never, ever, during your trials and testings.
When you saw only one set of footprints,
It was then that I carried you."

As the name implies, transcendent discipline transcends discipline. At this stage things become more effortless. This is because we are learning to live simply. And why have we learned simplicity? Because we have learned loving detachment, and as a result we are becoming more mindful as we continue the process of awakening. We know we have a soul and we know we are not alone. We know we are loved by our Creator, even if the One remains ineffable. For ineffability is the one truth which motivates humankind to pursue the human good. Within the simplicity of transcendent discipline we know the common good is what awaits all who yearn for it in both this world and the next.

We only have to glimpse back to gain perspective. Remember, when we or others we know were trapped in beguilement or defilement? If you have arrived at transcendent discipline, then you have come a long way. You have done a lot of hard work and experienced much personal growth during your period of noetic concentration. It is true that individuals may catch a glimpse of transcendent discipline on rare occasions at earlier stages, but it is rarely fully discerned or appreciated. Therefore, it does not grow. For anything to grow, it must be loved and watered in the spiritual reality of the universal baptisms of *Gnosis*.

As we experience transcendent discipline, we may be few in numbers, but we never feel alone. And as the world is still interested in the lesser manias of distraction, the soul transcends these attachments and knows it is one with the Creator. The noetic now begins his glorification. This is a blessed place to be. But it is not the end.

Tutelary Renewal
We will have conquered beguilement and sorted out our emotional defilements when we are open to the wisdom of noetic concentration. It therefore may seem logical to want to stay in a transcendent place of awareness and discipline. But this is not the end of the journey. In fact, there is no end to the soul's journey. There is only a newness of the soul being completely free to soar to greater and greater heights. In the spiritual world nothing remains motionless. Therefore, to stay in one place is just another form of beguilement.

However, when trapped in a beguiled mysticism we may feel the need to keep moving. This is when things become unsustainable. We pursue the next shiny thing to our detriment. For instance, in the material world individual growth can only continue until we reach maturity, and then it is sustained at that level. As a species, slow growth can continue as part of evolution, but personally our goal is to mature and sustain a healthy and harmonious lifestyle. What will then follow is the soul wanting to transcend the body, because in the spiritual domain growth continues forever and the soul can evolve quickly. But we must remember that growth in the material world is limited by the body. This is where we have to be careful in both the material and spiritual realms. In the material realm it is easy for the soul to become beguiled and pursue growth, which can only hurt the body and negatively affect the world. This can manifest as unnatural beguiled greed which has no understanding of itself. Today humanity is experiencing a beguiled world view, and as a consequence, greed has given rise to a mantra of unsustainable growth, which is exhausting the planet. The evidence is very clear, as we all are awakened to the spoils of climate change. The unnatural and unrealistic pursuit of continuous growth then becomes the cause of spoiled spiritualization. Herein rests the universal truth of motion. In the material world growth is limited, but in the spiritual world growth is unlimited, and confusing the two has drastic consequences for all life everywhere. We may have to resign to the fact that as a species we have materially evolved to the point of excess, and now we need to put more effort into maturing spiritually. With continued spiritual growth we will become more and more spiritualized. Can you imagine what the world would be like if humanity put more effort into spiritualization? This could mean the end to war, hunger, poverty, and the ushering in of global peace.

Naysayers may laugh at this as being naïve. But these same people also talk about artificial intelligence developing consciousness. Yes, we can have robotics, but as far as technology having any feelings, mindfulness, or self-awareness, it will not happen. Artificial intelligence is progressing, but artificial consciousness is not. There is zero progress on any miniscule level that will lead to robots or computers having a mind. Zero! Robots with consciousness do not exist, except in science fiction. This is another good example of beguiled mysticism. Science knows very little about how the mind works, let alone where it is located. However, mystics for centuries have been providing evidence of the existence of the mind that is being ignored by science because of its nebulous state. The nebulous gives birth to the luminous, which is the womb of spiritualization. As the human mind continues to evolve it will awaken to the beauty and power of Mother Earth, and humanity will continue to grow in our understanding of our own divine nature, as part of the One.

We need not feel sad for those who do not progress with us in this life. For this is also another form of beguilement. All we must remember is that they will have another opportunity in their next reincarnation to excel at attaining the human good. Until then do not become defiled by depression or the beguilements of materialization, but seek the spiritualization of loving kindness and pray always for the common good.

Henceforth in this life and in the next our tutelary guardians will always be watching over us. Just as the universe will continue to expand forever, so will our souls grow for an eternity. Therefore, always choose Oneness, and in doing so our soul will constantly be renewed. And in this renewal we will forever receive the gift of *Gnosis* from the One Holy Luminous Spirit.

The Gospel of Gnosis Commentary

Chapter One

The light of the One... Verses 1.1-1.2

The *Gospel of Thomas* has been dated by some to around 140-180 A.D. Other scholars say it is even older and date it prior to the *Gospel of Mark*. In the *Gospel of Gnosis* it is used as a greeting. Thomas is affectionately referred to as a friend and identified as an apostle who knew Jesus or Yeshua intimately and recorded his words for others to be stirred or awakened. The kingdom of heaven, which has escaped our present memory, can be rediscovered, if we search beyond the one tree of life found in *Genesis*. These verses tell us that whoever becomes acquainted with the five trees will not experience death. This suggests that life is more than one baptism and that each baptism denotes a stage of spiritual maturity.

Chapter Two

Chapter two begins by telling us that the future of humanity is self-determined by the individual and that the way of heaven is the way of meekness and peace.

The Ten Heavenly Laws... Verses 2.1-2.2

Happiness is found by correctly discerning the path you choose, which will result in life's mysteries being either revealed or veiled. Yeshua then discloses the new ten heavenly laws which surpass the old ten commandments. In the likeness of the beatitudes we are told to beware, or be aware of the living Christ within. The ten commandments of old are important laws, which support a mechanistic view of salvation. However, new heavenly laws encourage the individual to look beyond literalism and develop the deeper awareness of *Gnosis*. By comparison, the beatitudes tell us how to act to find peace, whereas the heavenly laws tell us what to be aware of to keep the peace we find.

1. Beware of the death of the body, which is here and ever present

The soul is given a physical home, but it is not its permanent resting place. Therefore, we must be aware of the trappings of the flesh, for the body will perish and what we accumulate on our earthly journey will only remain in spiritual form. As physical death may come to us at any moment, we must be vigilant and avoid all distractions which will keep us from completing our journey of absolute union with the One Great Spirit of Love.

2. Beware of how love drops to Earth as a leaf in fall, which no one can escape

Love is everything. Even as a leaf falls to the earth, it does not die. It will be reborn in its own heavenly image as eternal universal truth. For the truth is the treasure of omnipresent love.

A love which guides the soul to the eternal resting place we have come to call heaven. The soul which has attained love consciousness can exist and continue to love, and learn, and expand. For love cannot be quantified by matter and knows no limits or boundaries. For the soul which has found eternal love has been fully awakened to the beatific vision of Christ consciousness.

3. Beware of wealth, as it wanes like the moon

As the brightness of the moon is outshone by the sun, so, too, is the wealth of the world outshone by the brightness of a soul encompassing the loving embrace of the Great Spirit of love. For love actualized recognizes that the world is a place where the might and prosperity of material wealth never last.

4. Beware of the world of distraction which embodies the spirit

Distraction is like a moth which is deceived by the dim light of a candle and dives into it. Likewise, we must consider the world as a place where people steal from one another because of their beguiled values. All they accomplish is the pain of separation from the love of the Great Spirit.

5. Beware of exhaustion, which is the reward of wealth

Much of the breath of life is wasted on accumulating things, which only exhaust the body and spirit. In the end, people's possessions cannot save them, and when they pass, they will leave this world empty and lost.

6. Beware of desire, which weakens the spirit

Human sexuality is a gift from the Great Spirit. We have been blessed with this great gift to learn how to love God, as we love one another. Experiencing love in this way will bring us much happiness and fulfillment. However, the world has been infected with the disease of false intimacy and, like with any disease of the soul, we can become impacted in our body, mind and spirit.

7. Beware of indulgence, which casts confusion and doubt

Many people think of the world as a place of indulgence. The world offers many seductions designed to keep the soul imprisoned in darkness. The material world has much to sell and the competition to possess our soul is epidemic. To see the world through these eyes is like staring into a dirty looking glass—it keeps both the light of day and the light of *Gnosis* at bay.

8. Beware of worldly concerns which consume your vital spirit

Much time is wasted pursuing the seductions of the world which only waste away the hours and drain the body, mind and soul of its vital spirit. Life is not a game, and spiritual realities exist all around us. The more we live life as a game, the more our spirit is drained.

9. Beware of the outer search for truth

The world is a market place of religions and many shop around treating truth like chattel. As they pass through life rudderless, all they find is confusion and discontentment. Finally, after feasting on the outer world of religion, they become satiated. Once they have had their fill of disappointment, they begin to turn inward and find that the truth has always been within them, like a buried treasure waiting to be found. Here we learn that it is through life's higher challenges that higher truths are discovered.

10. Beware of the self, which deceives and helps no one

Without some awareness of the aforementioned nine heavenly laws, the world can become a place of victimization and self-deception. Even though human intention may be one of benevolence, altruism on its own will only keep the soul shrouded in a garment made of darkness. With the lack of *Gnosis*, the soul begins its earthly journey trapped in the self-righteous garment of ego-ridden materialism. As a result a person is actually deceiving themselves and helping no one. No amount of good intention can change the outcome.

Chapter Three

Parable of the Inn... Verses 3.1-3.2

The world is like an inn where you stay temporarily. None of the furniture is really yours. We will all be gone soon, for no one can stay long in an inn. Those who are self-serving do not take the resurrection seriously. They are concerned with the surface and their spirit is depleted, which causes them to rest before the time to rest has arrived. Their blindness leads them down paths of deception which causes the spirit to sleep, so when it awakens from its nightmare, it is afraid and lost.

This parable teaches us that the world is like an inn. It is temporary. We can enjoy it for a while, but sooner or later we have to check out. While we are here we can enjoy all the amenities. However, when we leave, we must leave all that belongs to the inn behind. This parable reminds us that we all live in a body, but sooner or later we have to leave it behind. For the world is attached to us, but we are not attached to the world.

It also teaches that ever since God created the material world for us to enjoy, the soul has wanted to be part of it. It wants to have a fine garment while in the world, but not at the cost of being lost within the illusions of materialism. This begs the question, what is a fine garment? Is it perfection, or is it the contrast we see in those whom the world shuns? This is why we must recognize that our continued spiritual growth is the most important task of the soul. Knowing this ensures the soul will not be seduced by the material world of greed. Overcoming greed, ignorance, and preparing to return to the heavenly realm is the second most important task of the soul. The first most important task is to learn to love one another in the material realm as a gift given to us by the Creator, so we can learn to love God more deeply and perfectly. As in the *Gospel of Luke* 10:27, this is another way to say, *"You shall love the Lord your God with all your heart and with all your soul and with all your strength and with all your mind, and your neighbor as yourself."* For as the soul spiritually matures, it must learn to overcome the seductions and illusions of the world. As the parable teaches us, we are only passing through the material world on our way back to the place from which we have originally come. Life in human form is short and we will all be called home soon. For no one can stay permanently at the inn.

Chapter Four

Parable of the Mountain Grove… Verses 4.1-4.3

There was a beautiful grove atop a mountain which cast a warm light on the forest below. Lovely and fragrant, it was said that it could satisfy any hunger or cure any illness. A sick and crippled man heard about this mountain but could not make the journey because the road was long and the mountain high. He yearned to go but could never fulfill his dream. But as he became sicker, he felt desperate and reached out to a close friend who was both wise and capable. The friend made ladders and cut steps in the mountain where needed. By pushing and pulling, the sick man was able to make it to the summit where he was immediately healed. When the man felt the healing he awakened to the love of Christ consciousness which had pulled and pushed him to the top of the mountain. He then knew it was his faith which healed him and not his presence atop the mountain. As he descended the mountain he made an offering of his life's pain to the Creator for the common good.

This parable offers us a way to find what we seek, even if we do not know what we are looking for. The cripple in the parable is asking for physical help, but also receives spiritual help from a close friend. This close friend is Yeshua or Jesus who provides the seeker not only with a physical ladder, but more importantly, a spiritual ladder. Since Jesus is identified as a close friend, He becomes known intimately as the inner realization of Christ consciousness. This can happen at any time and is known through direct experience of the One. This spiritual friend transcends any man-made religious institution with its various theologies and dogmas, and tells us that inner knowing is a natural gift of the natural world. The helper is a friend and not an institution. Too often we ignore our God given abilities and look outside of ourselves for answers. We ignore our own intuitions and search out the supernatural, which can result in further defilement of the divine mind. This tells us that the inner knowing and awareness of truth exist outside of institutions and the supernatural state. Community is the context in which we see the world, and as we learn to see the world through the spiritual eyes of Christ consciousness, we are awakened to our own spiritual identity. As a result, when we return to everyday life, we possess a new attitude towards grief and sorrow, and can now offer this misunderstood energy for God to use for the common good and the mutual benefit of all life.

Parable of a Mountain Covered With Forest… Verses 4.4-4.5

A follower asked Yeshua, "How can I be raised to eternal joy and peace?"
Yeshua answered, "It is only nothing that can give rise to something. If it
were any other way, then peace and joy would never be. Take, for example,
a mountain covered with a forest. The leaves and branches of the trees
spread shade everywhere. Surely, this mountain forest does not seek birds
and animals, but they all come on their own to nest and gather. Or think of
a great sea that draws all the rivers and springs and is vast without limits
and deep beyond measure. Surely, this ocean does not seek fish and scaly
creatures. But they all dwell there on their own. Those of you who seek
peace and joy are like these birds and fish. You need only soothe your minds
and live quietly. Then in practicing these teachings you will not have to seek
peace and joy, they will simply be there like the forest and the ocean. This
is how nothing gives rise to something."

Here a follower asked Yeshua, *"How can I be raised to eternal joy*
and peace?" And Yeshua answered, *"It is only nothing that can give*
rise to something. If it were any other way, then peace and joy would
never be." Yeshua knows this is difficult to comprehend, so he
provides a story to give his answer clarity.

Yeshua tells of a forest filled with birds and animals. He
also speaks of rivers and oceans which attract fish and scaly
creatures. This, he says, is how we should quiet our minds from
all distraction, so like these creatures we will not have to seek
peace and joy; it will simply be there waiting for us.

Chapter Five

Parable of the Way of Peace… Verses 5.1-5.2

The disciple then asked Yeshua, "How can I do nothing, but achieve everything?" Yeshua instructed the disciple to practice no desire, no action, no virtue and no truth to follow the way of peace. Again the disciple asked further of Yeshua for he did not understand. Yeshua answered, "For the last time I say, your heart seeks one thing after another, creating a multitude of problems. You must not allow them to flare up. For doing things out of dreariness is not part of your true being. Cast aside vainness and shallow experiences. Do not try to find pleasure by puffing yourself up through good deeds. Practice instead kindness and charity for all. Do not be concerned with the facts, forget about right and wrong, sinking or rising, winning or losing. Be like a mirror, for it reflects all desire, action, virtue, and truth. This is the way to find the Christ.

The follower is still confused, so Yeshua gives a further explanation, describing how to be raised to eternal peace and joy. Yeshua tells the follower to practice no desire, no action, no virtue, and no truth, to follow the way of peace. But the follower continues in their confusion. Like many of us, we do not possess the ability to comprehend spiritual truth because we remain asleep to the spiritual realities of the world. This is a world view to behold, as human kind longs for reconciliation through the transcendence of Christ consciousness. Finally, Yeshua expresses disappointment when he states, *"For the last time I say..."* As Yeshua senses the follower's helplessness, he explains himself in the following way:

No Desire
"To practice no desire means to not seek one thing after another which will only cause your heart to flare up." Here Yeshua is saying we should find the root of unhealthy desire, which keeps us from awakening to Christ consciousness. In this context, no desire is liberation from compulsion. For this type of desire is not truly coming from our authentic self. Compulsion comes from

beguilement, which is justified through human rationalization and denial of the Holy Spirit within. This is why scripture has called the sin against the Holy Spirit the only unforgivable sin. In other words, it is the greatest ignorance. Therefore, we condemn ourselves. So when the individual is overcome by false desire, they are like the drowning man who perceives the hand which is trying to pull him to safety as a hand which is pushing him under the waves. In this case unforgivable means to have made a choice based on ignorance; due to free will even the Holy Spirit will not compromise our right to choose. However, the good news is that we can change our mind if we choose to. But unfortunately, we will never change our minds unless we see through the ignorance. This is why community is so important. A community can support and pray for the ignorant, but in the end the decision rests with the individual. Hence it can be the greatest sin or the greatest ignorance. To try and eliminate all desire would be inhuman. However, by eliminating compulsive craving we make the choice to travel down the road of liberation, which leads to freedom.

No Action

"To practice no action means to not do things out of dreariness." Here Yeshua means to not be distracted. *"Doing things out of dreariness is not part of your true being."* Yeshua is saying, do not deceive yourself. Do not live your life swaying this way and that way. *"Cast aside vainness and shallow experiences. Do not try to find pleasure by puffing yourself up through good deeds."* To distance yourself from the material world, you must practice no action by neglecting what is not worthy or truly important, so that you can find your way home. Focus is a gift possessed by the authentic person. To be focused is to be Christ centered. Like the birds of the air, all our needs are provided for us through no efforts of our

own. This is why we get frustrated as we watch governments, businesses, religious institutions, and other sorted bureaucracies spin their wheels and accomplish very little. Today many people are busy, but many important things are not being done. No action means noticing what actions steal your time and which contribute to making life worth living.

No Virtue

"Practice instead kindness and charity for all." To practice no virtue means do not do things out of vanity. Instead, practice loving your neighbor. As the Earth humbly and quietly provides for all, so should we quietly and humbly provide for one another. This is the equanimity of faith realized as the fair distribution of wealth. So as Mother Earth freely shares her abundance for the welfare of all, so should we share our wealth for the betterment of one another. This is why the authentic person can say that happiness is found by living a virtuous life. For by living no virtue they have been liberated from the beguiled virtues of a self-serving ego. Therefore, no virtue means stilling the ego and living in the world without seeking the pride of good works. For these types of good works are born out of insecurity and narcissism, which will eventually expose the self-proclaimed guru in sheep's clothing. Here humility is the key. But humility does not mean becoming a slave or whipping post for another. For true humility means we have tamed the inner beguilements and defilements, which want to keep us imprisoned in ignorance. Therefore, a humble person is free, strong and has tamed the inner life of no virtue. No virtue means life is balanced and harmonious. Excessiveness is avoided, for this gives birth to false piety and humility.

No Truth

"Do not be concerned with the facts, forget about right and wrong, sinking or rising, winning or losing. Be like a mirror, for it reflects all." To practice no truth means to not be concerned with facts only. Forget about right and wrong and do not judge. Those who awaken to the truth see the world without judging. Be like a mirror, which only reflects back what is in front of it. It does not claim to possess knowledge of the truth, which it projects onto the world. Today we see many gurus, cults, religions, corporations, and governments compete for the truth. Each claims to hold the keys to the kingdom of truth. As a result, they promote confrontation and competition. No truth is like a mirror which leaves no copy of itself, and only reflects back cooperation and harmony. To practice no truth means to reject the subjectivity of dogma and the certitude of religiosity.

To practice no desire, no action, no virtue and no truth is the way to awaken to the way of Christhood. It offers sheeple who fear to stray from the steeple liberation from the anxieties of the competitive illusions of the world of stress and emotional defilement. This can be seen in the world as a resilient spirit shining forth as their soul radiates throughout the body.

Chapter Six

In traditional Christianity there is one baptism at birth. Some people will wait until adulthood, whereas others may want to be baptized again and again as they join different churches. There are even other non-Christian groups which ask that individuals be un-baptized, if they want to join their particular organization. However, whatever form it takes, baptism usually signifies a purifying experience or initiation. However, the *Gospel of Gnosis* tells us there are many baptisms and that each baptism is not so much an initiation, but a recognition that the individual has progressed from one state of consciousness to the next higher level of consciousness, all of which leads to purer climaxes of *Gnosis*.

First Baptism: Release From Beguilement... Verses 6.1-6.3

This baptism can also be called beguiled mysticism. For as we have discussed, the soul seeks its return to the Creator through mysticism. By the same token, the shadow side seeks to implement a phantom mysticism to beguile the soul.

Verse 6.1

When Adam and Eve ate from the tree of knowledge, they became enrobed and rejected the power of the demiurge and a sleep fell over their hearts and minds.

This does not mean they felt shame, as mentioned in the *Genesis* interpretation; it means they became self-aware and enlightened. They rejected the false god or demiurge of the bible. As a result, the demiurge became angry and banished Adam and Eve from the garden. When they were banished, a trance or sleep fell over them. This is the beguilement of the soul.

However, each day of daily struggle slowly awakened them from a trance and the scales of seduction began to fall from their eyes. The light of day burned their eyes anew and the purification of mankind began and shall continue until the end of time.

This can be interpreted that no matter how much distraction a soul will face, it can never completely forget or lose its connection to the one true God. Therefore, as Eve and Adam worked and toiled, they slowly awakened from the trance placed on them by the demiurge. They became reborn as the internal light of God burned their eyes anew. This has been the journey of our earthly mother and father and will be the journey of each person born thereafter until the end of time. This tells us that we all have our individual and unique path to follow, as we strive for the *Gnosis* which will guide us to Christ consciousness.

Verse 6.2

A wolf in sheep's clothing was sent to devour the truth of mankind. Those who seek rest are seduced into an early sleep and are in peril of an eternal sleep that does not refresh. Those who awaken to the misery of such defilement are set on the path of righteousness. This is the first baptism of the catechumen, which releases him from the darkness of beguilement whose root is in the circle of trees which encompass Paradise.

Since the demiurge or false god has been outfoxed, it has sent its unholy spirit to prey on humankind as a wolf in sheep's clothing. This wolf uses the illusion of false mysticism to herd souls. As a result, many are beguiled and the illusion seduces humanity into an early trance, which is like sleep. And as they awaken from this sleep upon death of the physical body, they are not refreshed. What they awaken to is an abused consciousness that lacks Divine awareness and wisdom. They are therefore lost and dominated by a fear that will rule their afterlife. However, those who awaken to the misery of a beguiled mysticism through *Gnosis* are prepared to begin life everlasting in the presence of the Divine Mind of God. To awaken from beguiled mysticism is to receive the first baptism of the catechumen. The catechumen is now awakened to his root which is in heaven. For he is now aware that the Garden of Eden has spread from a root which is encompassed within Paradise.

Verse 6.3

From the beginning the spirit which now dwells in the psyche originated from the water of life. The first strand that enslaves is broken by this baptismal blessing.

All life originates from water, just as all spiritual blessings in a physical body come from our first baptism through water. This is the first step of the catechumen towards the light of *Gnosis*. The first strand that enslaves is the original trance we have received from the demiurge. This baptism by water breaks the hold the original trance has over the soul. The soul of the catechumen is enrobed by the Holy Spirit as it now begins the journey of awakening from ignorance. To become enrobed is to begin the ritual of crossing over from a trance state to becoming a seeker of *Gnosis*.

Second Baptism: Release from Defilement... Verses 6.4-6.11

If ignorance is bliss, it is because emotional defilement is perpetual and will never abandon us. This is why this stage of our evolution can be the most difficult. Our emotions are used by the shadow to manipulate us. This is why we see many illnesses on the rise, especially illnesses like depression. In our so-called civilized society, it is safe to say that depression is epidemic. When we are emotionally defiled, our thoughts and feelings can be used to completely possess us. As a result we experience maladies like anxiety, depression, and suicide, just to name a few. Sadly, illness will continue to prosper if the second baptism from defilement is not activated within us. This type of trance is just another form of abuse, which can and will be inflicted on us from many sources. Some of the major causes of such a trance are gurus, cults, corporations, and religious institutions. As we are seduced by our defiled emotions, not only are we susceptible to abuse by others, but we are also predisposed to abusing ourselves. The only saving grace is that when we hurt enough we instinctively look for a way out of our pain, and this is the opposite of what the demiurge expects. The demiurge does not expect this because it has no idea what love is and therefore has no understanding of the power of love. Once our soul seems to be broken, it can suddenly look very deeply within itself and find the reserves it needs to overcome the trance and begin to awaken from its sleep.

It is at this time that the soul holds onto the only thing it has left—it holds onto ineffable love. In its dark cell, which is the body, it finds a calm still light within itself. In the words of the mystic John of the Cross, we enter into the dark night of the soul. This is the alarm clock of the psyche which nobody can explain. It is the beginning of the end of emotional defilement. This is what it means to be reborn and awaken to a new life. However, once we are awakened from the gripping effects of the trance, it is easy to fall asleep again, if we are not vigilant. We must remember at this stage that the journey back to wholeness is not clear to the soul. The soul will have to face many trials and tribulations, because the demiurge is very angry and will not give up its goal of possessing the soul. The path the soul must now follow is unique. Each soul has its own journey which at times may intersect with other souls. But for the soul to awaken to its true essence, it must remain faithful to its calling.

The soul will continue to face many diversions on this journey, and in the stage of emotional defilement the battle within can be most fierce. This will manifest itself in what we call old-fashioned denial or emotional blocking. It is caused by defiled logic, which is used to rationalize ignorance. This type of ignorant bias is very easily identified as bigotry, intolerance, discrimination, and xenophobia. After all, why not project onto others our own inner disturbances so we can sleep soundly?

Verse 6.4

The Holy Spirit comes for the second time in the likeness of a female. Just as in the pangs of the parturient the time for Gnosis *approaches.*

Here the Holy Spirit is identified with the feminine and the trance of ignorance has been exposed. *Gnosis* is now free to increase, but can only do so through the pains of birthing new life. For as we know, the pursuit of awareness is a hard road which many begin to follow, but few are able to complete. The reason for the diversion can be promptly laid at the feet of emotional defilement. For one thing, evolution has taught humanity that it is not the intelligent or strong who survive, it is the most adaptable. So for this reason many outsmart themselves and continue to follow the road of ignorance.

Verse 6.5

Those seduced begin to feel the burning of desire that leaves man needing more. Lost in the defilement of their own darkness, a glimmer of light faintly burns on the horizon.

As the soul struggles to keep awake, it is constantly being seduced by desire. This desire manifests in many ways, which are all the distractions of an artificial world. The soul must use wisdom to discern what is healthy and what is not. Some obvious distractions are those which can seduce en mass. However, for the truly stoic individual there is always the old standby of pride and piety. The shadow side of humanity can and will use anything at its disposal, which means any virtue can be turned into a vice.

There is a way to awaken from this sleep. We are told that when we feel the burning of desire that leaves us wanting more, we are on the doorstep of ignorance. To use addiction as an example, there comes a time when the source of our desire will abandon us and the freedom we seek will be turned into the slavery of obsession. If we only had the courage to open the door and look within, we would find a light that still faintly burns, because we are never truly abandoned by the true source of all life. The light of the Creator of all burns on the horizon of life, and we can choose to follow it. This is the second baptism of the neophyte who is now willing to receive the deeper cleansing of receiving.

Verse 6.6

With each motion towards the light, the light also moves toward a greater light. With each movement the light becomes brighter, but comes no closer until the appointed time. In the darkness the light shines on the face of evil and the Archigenetor is angered because its beauty is being lost.

With each step we take toward the light, it moves simultaneously toward a greater light. This tells us that the light is not running away like the demiurge would have us think. Here the demiurge tries to convince us that we are being deceived to fuel anger within us, so we will blame the One true God for all our suffering. But the truth is, we are not being deceived. Rather, the light is leading us back toward a greater light which is the true home of the soul. Here we learn to understand love and search for it. And when we find it, nothing can compare with it and we receive it forever. For a love embraced can never be lost, even in the midst of further emotional defilements at the hands of the demiurge. For now the soul has glimpsed the path home and has recovered its fate.

The soul will continue to open itself to the process of life amidst all its struggles. Here we come to awaken to the knowledge that the light will grow brighter and brighter and at the appointed time, whether long or short, hard or easy, we can shed ignorance completely and become fully awakened to Christ consciousness.

Verse 6.7

This is the washing which awakens the neophyte to the future resurrection.

As we continue to grow in *Gnosis*, ignorance falls away by the power of self-knowledge. The road may continue to be hard, especially in the beginning. The shadow will never surrender, so vigilance becomes even more vital for the revival of the soul. However, as we continue to awaken, the life within will develop more purpose and meaning. Now that we have a deeper understanding of emotional defilement, when we fall, the pain may be even greater than when we were blinded by the ignorance of a beguiled mysticism. For now we know the wrong we have committed and are tempted to regress back into beguilement to hide our faces from pain. But because we have grown in the light of meaning and purpose, we can now choose to get back up, and continue on our journey as a neophyte, all the while receiving the faith of this second baptism as we are washed clean of emotional defilement.

Third Baptism: Release From Deception… Verses 6.8-6.11

Now that the soul is awakening from its emotional defilements, it prepares itself to enter into the third baptism, within which it will be released from deception. This waking up from deception manifests itself in what can be called noetic concentration. This is a self-discipline that extends beyond the ordinary, even beyond our own strength. The soul begins to hear the calling of discipleship more clearly, as it identifies with the inner light of wisdom.

Verse 6.8

The third baptism awakens us to a sound that is foreign to us. We do not recognize it or know from whence it comes. It comes to put fear in our midst and mourning in our hearts. For now we shall mourn most bitterly. As for the future, let us make our flight before we are imprisoned once again and dragged into the bosom of the underworld.

Here we are awakened to a sound which is new. We receive the good news, but now hear it differently. We hear differently because the soul has been purging itself from defilement. As a result, we experience fear and urgency, while at the same time experiencing grief and intimacy. These emotions are real and are not tainted by defilement. We not only receive the light, but want to live by it. All the burdens of an unhealthy lifestyle lose their seductive powers over the soul. We come to know more deeply that we must continue to seek wisdom, or risk being once again dragged back into beguiled mysticism.

Verse 6.9

For when we hear the voice which calls us forth, we follow it through the darkness and become enthroned and elevated to noetic heights. For the loosening of our bondage is upon us, and the times are cut short, and the days are shortened as our time is fulfilled. We grow from a tree which has its root in heaven. The tree which has no leaves and produced only the fruit of ignorance has its boughs broken by truth and the harvest of ignorance passes away.

Now, as we respond to our calling, we take on the challenges of living our faith, which guides the soul through darkness. The soul now begins to develop a transcendent discipline which provides us with an inner discipline or strength, surpassing what we can do on our own. For human willpower is finite, but a transcendent discipline rooted in wisdom is infinite.

As we accept this new transcendent discipline, we are delivered to a higher knowledge of the noetic. As a noetic, we are protected from the darkness of the shadow and become enthroned within the mantle of grace. Our time of suffering may not be over, but it begins to pale with the joy we now feel, as ignorance has its boughs broken. This breaking of the boughs of ignorance is a grace realized by the soul as it follows its root back to the tree which has its root in heaven. This is the effect of the higher knowledge of Christ consciousness which connects all souls. For the tree of ignorance has no leaves, which demonstrates that it has a shallow root which cannot exist in the infertile soil of a lower beguiled mind.

Verse 6.10

When the disciple is given to the light of goodness, darkness fears the future. For behold, even as the Archigenetor hears for itself the sound of truth for the first time, it has no comprehending. It seeks the truth for itself, but has no understanding of it and has no choice but to call forth all its depraved powers to crucify the disciple of the Lamb of God.

Now that the soul has become totally resistant to the shadow of the Archigenetor, or the incarnation of evil, it is subjected to the truth. However, evil cannot comprehend the truth so it becomes more afraid and desperate. It can only do what it knows how to do. Evil, therefore, calls forth its greatest power, which is to persecute Christ and all the disciples of Christ consciousness.

Verse 6.11

As the disciple is still weak, he must pray for the guidance of the Holy Spirit and trust in the One true light which calls him forth.

Here the disciple of Christ will be faced with his or her greatest challenges. This is where all weakness must be purged or the disciple may return to a beguiled mysticism, or become emotionally defiled to such an extent that their progress will be damaged. However, this fate does not have to come to pass. For the soul that possesses some weakness can still make progress, if it calls on the One true light within which is the Holy Spirit. In these moments of attack the Archigenetor is once again trying to regain possession of the soul. To win this very ferocious battle, the soul that calls on the One will recognize the Holy Spirit in places it has never seen it before. Through this interior battle with evil, the soul will be awakened to a deeper Christ consciousness and find God in the faces of other souls whom it meets on humanity's journey of awakening. For as the soul is now attracted to kindred spirits, intimacy and love burn so profoundly that evil cannot be in its presence. This love among many souls will now prepare the soul for the fourth baptism.

Fourth Baptism: Release From Ignorance... Verses 6.12-6.15

Verse 6.12

Now behold! All natures, all formed things, all creatures and their comforts, on their own and together, will be resolved into their own roots. This is why you become sick and die, because you love what deceives you. You become like the thing you love. Be careful that no one deceives you and may peace be within you. Be careful that no one leads you astray with, "Come over here," *or* "Go there." *Follow only the child within.*

Here the noetic is asked to concentrate on the distractions of the soul. For at the root of each problem their fate can be found. If it is the root of ignorance, then ignorance will be their fate. If it is the root of *Gnosis,* then this will be their destiny. For we become like the thing we love, and each problem will bring its own rewards. To follow the child within tells us that each soul has its beginning, which is pure. To follow the inner voice of purity is to follow the root which comes from a transcendent discipline.
Verse 6.13

Those who seek peace will find it and will want to share it among their brethren. The child with the peace of Christ consciousness will be granted the mysteries of the one voice revealed through the wisdom of Sophia.

As the noetic becomes more intimate with wisdom, he will share what he knows for the benefit of all sensate life. As the soul retraces its steps, it can now return to the purity of childhood, which was taken from it through its beguilement. As the eyes of Christ consciousness are opened wider, the soul comes to know wisdom more intimately by her feminine name Sophia.

Verse 6.14

The voice of the perfect intellect will become the foundation for the All. What was once hidden will be glorified within them. For the One is both mother and father and copulates with itself. Therefore it is not authentic to not know yourself. Examine yourself that you may know yourself, that you may understand who you are, in what way you exist and how you will come to be. For it is not fitting that you remain ignorant of yourself. For they who have not known themselves have known nothing, but those who come to know themselves have at the same time already achieved knowledge about the depth of the One.

Here we are told that the perfect intellect, or wisdom, becomes the foundation for our relationship with God. As a result, we will continue to grow, and Christ consciousness will be glorified in us.

The One copulates with itself, symbolizing union and the singular point of creation. God is now comprehended as transgendered—both male and female. To not know oneself is to ignore the existence of the soul, and to fall into the beguilement of living the unexamined life. Therefore, to not know yourself is to not know God, whereas to know God is to also know yourself.

For the soul which does not pursue self-knowledge will know nothing and remain ignorant. The power of ignorance can condemn the soul to death, or at least to many reincarnations.

Verse 6.15

Every noetic seeking and longing will find what they are looking for. And the eternal Holy Spirit will soothe, protect and love your essence back to fulfillment within the One true androgynous God. These are the glories which await the faithful who cast aside the garment of ignorance, for where the nous *is, there rests all the beauty of Paradise.*

As the soul develops noetic concentration, it is awakened more and more to *Gnosis*. The soul has now evolved to a place of confidence and certainty that embraces the wisdom of Sophia. Through Sophia the soul's ability to merely transcend discipline is surpassed. The noetic seeker will become more fully awake to the fulfillment that awaits the soul as it prepares to return to the presence of the One true androgynous God. At this time the soul receives everlasting confirmation that where the *nous* is, there rests the beauty of paradise. Here the *nous* is identified with the mind, which is now prepared to move onto the next baptism—release from consumption.

Fifth Baptism: Release From Consumption... Verses 6.16-6.19

Verse 6.16

Stripped of the garments of ignorance and clothed in the light which casts no shadow, nothing will appear that belongs to the powers of the Archons. The time arrives when darkness will dissolve and ignorance will die. The bondage of the lesser has no sight in the presence of brilliance. However, a barb remains until the resurrection to remind us of the realm of giants.

At this time the soul has transcended many of the seductions of the material world. It has no desire to consume anything which is not necessary for its continued existence in the physical body. It has reached the evolutionary state known as tutelary renewal. In this state, through *Gnosis*, the soul has stripped away many of the garments of the flesh. Ignorance has very little influence, if any, and the world is seen and experienced through the light which casts no shadow. This light shines from within and is a centering force of the Holy Spirit. However, even though darkness has no root, in the brilliance of the internal light the soul is aware that as long as it still lives within the physical body, it will have a barb or thorn in its flesh. This barb is left to remind us that while we are still on this Earth, the giants, or evil spirits, will continue to roam looking for souls to seduce.

Verse 6.17

As they prepare to meet in the fullness of the eternal kingdom all brethren will gather and proclaim the ineffable through the power of the Holy Spirit with the renewal of Christ consciousness.

As souls awaken, they will gravitate to other awakened beings to meet in the eternal kingdom of Christ consciousness. They will share their wisdom with those who are still searching, and as they continue to embrace the ineffability of the Holy Spirit, their renewal of Christ consciousness will continue. This is the meeting place of bodhisattvas and saints.

Verse 6.18

Tutelary renewal remains inexpressible to every sovereignty and every ruling, except to the children of the light. The sovereigns who resign to the greater good truly learn to love their neighbors as themselves and leave a great gift upon the altar of peace.

As the soul awakens to spiritual realities, it is protected by tutelary spirits. It has chosen to completely renew itself through reconciliation with the One true God. The children of light will surpass those who do not possess *Gnosis* and offer their lives on the altar of peace to help others. They will make a gift of their pain so others can receive the healing energy of Christ consciousness. This is their great gift—pain converted into the energy of love, which can be utilized by all seekers.

Verse 6.19

Our teacher, Yeshua, instructs those who wish to find the treasure of Paradise within to approach the altar of peace by passing through the gate along the narrow path of Christhood. The one who knows is called forth to serve the Prince of Peace, first as a disciple, and then as an elder who knows the will of the One and prepares to enter through the gates of Paradise. The elder who prepares for the resurrection rejects the power of kingship and embraces the authority of the Prince of peace.

Here, under the protection and guidance of tutelary renewal, intimacy with Yeshua overflows. Through a personal relationship with the One, a soul finds the Christ within and has the courage and fervency to follow the path less travelled. The disciple, who says yes to the call of service, is now given the keys to Paradise and is branded as an elder by Yeshua, the Prince of Peace. As the love of *Gnosis* continues to grow brighter and brighter, the energy of peace embraces the soul and prepares it for the final resurrection. Until now the soul has experienced a number of baptisms and resurrections. However, as the final resurrection approaches, the soul prepares itself to be liberated from the garment of the body.

Chapter Seven

The Resurrection of Truth… Verses 7.1-7.2

Some people want to become learned. That is their purpose when they begin to solve unsolved problems. If they succeed, they are proud. But they have not stood in the word of truth. Rather, they seek their own rest, which we receive from our savior and our lord, the Christ. We receive rest when we come to know the truth and rest within it. What, therefore, is the truth about the resurrection? For many do not believe in it, and few find it. So how does the One open the eyes of those who wish to come to know the resurrection?

The resurrection is not a one-time event. It can happen many times during our life within the body. This, of course, culminates with the final resurrection, once the soul is liberated from the physical body at death. But many do not follow this path of knowledge due to an enlarged ego, and pursue other diversions, which are void of spiritual realties. Therefore, those who wish to know the resurrection must open their eyes, reject ignorance, and envision the non-corporeal spiritual reality of authentic truth.

The Vision of the Blind Servant... Verse 7.3

A man went before his master for stealing a loaf of bread to feed his family. When asked by his master whether he was guilty of stealing the loaf, the man said no. When asked if he denied taking the loaf, the man said he had indeed taken the loaf. Since the man had no defense but his own, he was asked to give a good reason for his actions. The man stated that taking the loaf was not a theft because he took it out of his need and not his want. He then accused his master of neglecting his workers while he and his family would eat to excess. To this the master replied in judgement that as we are seen in this world, so do we clothe ourselves. He then sentenced the man to death and his family to labor.

This parable tells us that unbalanced power always results in the need for greed to control the masses. The desire for power and control has always been a problem, the result of which can be seen in the disproportionate distribution of the Earth's resources. Those in power might possess a bright intellect, but may very well be lacking in the wisdom of Sophia. Thus, they are easily seduced by greed, and as a result, must constantly be creating want and need in the masses. In this parable the theft of a loaf by a man in need becomes the main teaching point.

When the accused thief states that he has not stolen the loaf, he shines a light on the opulence of the master who has set himself up as judge and jury. As the accused states his case, and tells his master he had taken the loaf because of his need, the master responds with a lack of compassion and no ability to relate to the significance of the imbalances of power established by the master's greed.

Since the master is blinded by greed, when he passes sentence on his slave, he inadvertently passes sentence on himself. This is expressed as the master states, *"As we are seen in this world, so do we clothe ourselves."*

The Swallowing of Death... Verses 7.4-7.5

When the man faced his executioner, he was given a vision of how he had been seen in this world. He saw his flesh worn like an old garment that had become torn and worn out. For how we are seen in this world we wear like a garment. Then the savior revealed to him the sunset of his life and held him in his arms as he was drawn into the One by beams of radiant light. Then, as the executioner's hand fell, he was drawn to heaven by the sun, on what appeared to be beams of light and nothing could hold him down. All that remained was his garment. This is the resurrection of the spirit, which swallows up the flesh. So as the world is clothed, so will it be judged.

When the soul enters this material world, it puts on the physical body like a garment. This garment is bound by earthly laws where the soul is bound by spiritual laws. Over time the garment will decay, whereas the soul will eventually bc freed from the restrictions of the body. However, during the time the soul spends in the body it will have to deal with human limitations. At the moment of death the soul will overcome the limitations of forethought and afterthought. For how the soul is seen in the world, it wears like a garment. In other words, while the soul exists in the physical world it must suffer the restrictions of both body and mind. However, at the moment of physical death the soul awakens from the drunkenness of darkness and will cast off the fetters of forgetfulness. As *Gnosis* fully penetrates ignorance, beams of light will penetrate the soul, and liberate it completely from the body. Then all that will remain for the human eye to gaze on is a worn lifeless garment. *So as the world is clothed, so will it be judged.* Here we can take comfort that it is good to wear a different garment than what the world asks us to conform to. We may find it hard to live in a world according to its value systems, but if we can continue to live according to our authentic self, then we can also be judged separately from the world.

The Superior Way... Verses 7.6-7.8

In the beginning a course may be followed that espouses a slight deviation with every advancement that continuously provides greater room for error. Our concern is not to be sinless, but to be one with God. Thus the self-knower is a double person. There is the part which he understands by rules and standards within itself. However, there is also the other part and its understanding has become something new throughout. It has struggled to become a superior being.

Now, as the soul continues to advance, it will learn the good, which this world can provide when centered on God. As we are justified by God, we learn to accept the good with the bad as part of the journey of life. Then we realize that we should not focus on perfection, which is a distraction, but rather when we focus on God, our perfection becomes possible. As a result, we are aware of the double life of a soul trapped in a body. We can now straddle the laws of both the physical and spiritual worlds, as we learn each life lesson given to us. Thanks to this new awareness, the soul can commit to the superior way, which is made up of the spiritual realities of *Gnosis*.

Verses... 7.9-7.11

This latter part knows itself as no longer man, but at one with the Divine Mind. This is the spirit in motion, as it passes from one act to another.

The lesser part must work towards the evolution of its being. Only thus can it reproduce the higher. Something exists within, which is higher than the self. Eternity calls forth life to repose, complete itself, and become endless. For within itself many things are engraved to be held by the eternal engraver.

As the human soul progresses, it now identifies more with the Divine Mind than with the human mind. The human soul is now aware that it is a spirit in motion, and can never stop pursuing the good at the peril of being overcome by darkness. Constant growth is the reward of the higher self, and is the only reward it seeks. Now, with every new small awareness, the soul receives greater and greater peace and repose. For now the ineffable truth of the Creator is engraved on its heart and *Gnosis* is the only way to decipher it.

Verse 7.12

There is no injustice when a man suffers due to the condition he finds himself in. We cannot ask to be happy when our actions have not earned us happiness. The good are happy because they are good. For happiness is only found in living the virtuous life. When the seekers discover virtues' divine purpose, they will be raised above the crowds.

Even while still in the garment of the body, the soul can begin to transcend the physical, and glimpse more and more the gates of eternity. This delivers the soul to a knowing which surpasses all it has known to this point. Whether by vision, or rapture, the soul now desires to be free of its garment, and the mistakes of the past have lost the power to confuse or condemn. The soul now knows without a doubt that the miserable are miserable because they chose not to be virtuous, while the happy are happy because they chose to live a virtuous life. And when the soul discovers the virtuous life, its divine purpose is revealed, and it will grasp why others who are still possessed by the lower self are bewildered. Having transcended emotional defilement, they feel the pain that others are oblivious to, and lean forward into the future with joy in their hearts.

Chapter Eight

Parable of a Slave… Verse 8.1

Yeshua said, "All have the ability to awaken, yet do not know it. Many prefer to drift on a great sea chained to an oar and suffer a lifetime as a slave. You are ignorant of what you possess and are chained to the oar which has been set below."

All souls have the ability to awaken to *Gnosis,* but not everyone chooses to do so. Some prefer to float through life adrift on a great sea of ignorance, at the same time offering themselves as slaves to be abused by the master of darkness. As a result, the chains of ignorance repetitiously enslave them as life cycles around them. Since they fear to look at what is below the surface of their limited self-awareness, they remain ignorant and do not know what is passing them by. They prefer the seductions of a lower primitive existence, and do not realize that when their lower-self dies, their soul will be set adrift among the lost. For how can a soul which has pursued darkness awaken to light without first being purified by the process of reincarnation?

The Tree With Seven Limbs… Verses 8.2-8.9

Verse 8.2

Yeshua spoke, "Each season, a tree with seven large limbs grows. It becomes stronger and sends out new shoots. It is not something that happens once and is complete. It is growing all the time. So it must be with you."

The tree of life has seven limbs. Each limb corresponds to different elevated states of awareness. The stages are: Stillness, Call, Transition, Grace, Revelation, Transformation and Transfiguration. The tree with seven limbs symbolizes the journey towards complete spiritualization. As we learn to live a more spiritualized life, we become stronger and more connected to one another and the Divine essence of the Creator, which is present in all forms of life. As the seasons turn, so are we elevated within the Divine circles of life. Both here and in the hereafter we will always be called upon to grow and evolve. The journey never ends; it only continues to grow in love, which has no limit and will never end.

First Limb… Verse 8.3

The first limb offers repose from the heat of the day. If we sit long enough in its shade, we will remember. When we begin to remember, we will never forget our root and the relationship with what has been lost will continue, as we rise to our feet and climb.

Stillness
Stillness comes to us in the quiet of the present moment. Just think of the Buddha who quite literally sat under a tree until he experienced enlightenment. This is a good example of how

a human being can obtain enlightenment, if they can still themselves. Over his life span the Buddha continued to grow in his awakened state. For enlightenment, once achieved, will never reach an end. Like love, it will continue to grow in this life and the next. Yeshua also grew in wisdom throughout his life, and his path of enlightenment became a gift to all humanity, known as Christ consciousness. Yeshua was nailed to a tree and as his essence mingled with all creation, he became one with the Creator and the created. So, whether we literally make a decision to sit under a tree, or simply accept the tree motif, the result can be the same. We will begin our heavenly journey of *Gnosis.*

Second Limb... Verse 8.4

The second limb will reveal the leaves which return to the earth and become part of our future. As the buds of the tree reveal themselves, minds are raised to the questions of life.

Call

A still mind is open to the call of humility. This call will ask the mind to continue on its search, as it ascends the tree of life. As we embrace the tree of life and begin to climb upwards, we will notice its leaves falling to the ground. This symbolizes the cycles of rebirth, as the leaves fall to the ground and become part of the tree's root, which helps provide nourishment. As we ascend, we begin to suckle the spiritual nourishments which sustain our soul. We are called to explore the way of luminosity by all the small and little deaths in our life. With each ending there is a new beginning.

Third Limb… 8.5

The third limb produces the fruit of faith, which encourages stamina and endurance to continue the ascent.

Transition

As we mature from one state to the next, we may feel tremendous joy or tremendous sadness. These feelings of consolation and desolation are the markers of progress. For a soul to progress, it must be in a state of flux, and experience both aridity and abundance. Here the soul will realize the dangers inherent in trusting in its own strength. This is also how we grow in charity and virtue. As a gardener plants a tree and watches it grow, so too does a soul grow. As the tree grows, we grow with it. The tree survives as it endures through all the elements, because it is rooted in the soil provided by the Creator. As the tree grows, it becomes strong. And as the soul grows, it, too, becomes strong.

Fourth Limb… Verse 8.6

The fourth limb produces the fruit of spiritual ease and restfulness, which is awakened from the worries of the world.

Grace

As the tree which is watered grows, so, too, does the soul which is watered with life giving grace and spiritual consolations. This is the tipping point where the soul experiences a complete *metannoia* and a growing commitment to spiritual conversion. As the soul continues its ascent, it is now gaining evidence of the duality, which it is now awakening from. This is the beginning of the soul's liberation from the garment of the body. Through grace it now recognizes the enticements of the material realm, and discerns a future free from the anxious worries of the world.

Fifth Limb... Verse 8.7

The fifth limb produces the fruit of ecstasy with a view of the beauty beyond the hills, where joy and happiness await.

Revelation

The soul is still in the body, but now that it has ascended the tree of life to this fifth limb, it has a new revelatory view of the world. The soul now recognizes the existence of others for what it is. The beauty of the world can be seen beyond the misery inflicted by the demiurge. As such, the world and its usefulness is put into perspective. This vision of what awaits beyond the hills brings the soul much joy and happiness.

As the heart of knowledge is stretched, the soul is awakened to a deeper self-awareness. Here a radical transformation occurs, in which the eyes of the soul now see beyond intellectual visions.

Sixth Limb... Verse 8.8

The sixth limb finds stillness from the rustling of leaves where the voice of Gnosis *can be heard.*

Transformation

As the climber looks upward, he can now catch a glimpse of the future. He can see beyond the sky and stars. He now gazes on the gates of eternity, which is waiting for the spiritual sojourner. The soul experiences a union of body, mind and soul, and feels the presence of God through the stillness of the awakened spirit of *Gnosis*. God is experienced in a new way, which transcends the body, and sees beyond the veil of divine consciousness. The soul is now being pulled out of itself and beyond itself. This is the mystical transformation from *perichoresis* to *quaternity*, wherein the soul experiences the spiritual delights of unitive love.

Seventh Limb… Verse 8.9

The seventh limb produces the fruit of wisdom where one rests in the arms of true love.

Transfiguration

As the soul can climb no further, it sits atop the tree of life, and does not take its gaze off the heavens. In its silence the face of God is like the breeze. And as the tree blossoms, the soul may find within itself the fruit of ecstasy. Here the soul will wait in the arms of love until its appointed time. At this time the soul will be united with the Divine, just as two flames are joined as one, or the rain joins with the sea. This is the final transfiguration of the soul, as it is consumed in complete union with Christ consciousness.

Chapter Nine

The Destiny of Humans… Verses 9.1-9.6

As we consider these verses, we can conclude that they evolved around the Passover meal—the Last Supper with Yeshua. At some point Yeshua is once again questioned, this time by the one who loved him—probably the Apostle John. John is a significant person in the life and narrative of Yeshua and in the

Gnostic tradition the *Gospel of John* is the most favored of all the canonical gospels.

Verse 9.1

Yeshua was again questioned by the one who loved him most, who asked, "Will all souls be led into the pure light?" The Master then replied, "These are great matters that have risen in your mind and are difficult to explain to anyone except those of the unshakable race."

The unshakable race are those who cannot be seduced or dominated. They recognize their lineage. Because they cannot be bought or sold, they will rise to greatness through the living light of Christ consciousness. As a result, they become the elders who are the protectors and teachers of the good news. This has been the fate and fortune of those who remain centered on the truth. Truth and justice are noble causes for the seeker of *Gnosis.*

Verse 9.2

"Those upon whom the Holy Spirit of the living will descend and whom the spirit will empower will be saved and become perfect and worthy of greatness and be cleansed of all evil and the anxieties of wickedness. For those who refuse to embrace an anxious world worry not for the incorruptible and must concern themselves from this moment on without anger, jealousy, envy, desire, or greed for anything."

Being human offers each life challenges, which can either support or hinder personhood. A home is therefore created for the soul while living in the flesh. Those who choose to live the life of a true human being do so in the knowledge that they have overcome evil and the world of deception. They are not seduced by wickedness, or oppressed into slavery by the anxieties of anger, jealousy, envy, desire, or greed. For these are manifestations of an ignorant, senseless spirit. Free will is always a choice between life and lifelessness. To make ourselves lovable is to freely love and be loved.

Verse 9.3

It is therefore not as Moses spoke. Adam did not fall into a sleep, but rather this trance-like state was a loss of sense. Thus the mind becomes sluggish that it may not understand or discern.

Moses spoke wrongly, because he was the inheritor of the demiurge which delivered him unto ignorance, and a false presumption of reality. The truth is that Adam and Eve did not fall asleep, but were awakened to the reality of the One. This was incomprehensible to the demiurge, who vainly curses humankind and the spiritual realities of creation.

However, ignorance is a curse, which humankind can transcend by waking up to the senses. Therefore, the greatest ignorance is not a function of the intellectual, but a function of the mind. The mind, which awakens from the ignorance of the senses, awakens to the emotional and feeling nature of the soul. This emotional intelligence far surpasses the intellect, and is the mother of enlightened bliss. Therefore, the greatest ignorance is not a lack of intellectual prowess; the greatest ignorance is the lack of emotion.

Verses 9.4-9.5

Before the washing of feet the Master lastly received one more question from the one who loved him. "Where will the souls go when they leave their

*flesh?" With this the Master laughed and said, "The soul in which there
is more power than the contemptible spirit is strong.. She escapes from evil
and through the intervention of the incorruptible one she is saved and taken
up to eternal rest."*

Even in the face of corruption, Yeshua's laugh represents the
paradox of enlightenment. His laugh is not meant to mock, but
to shine light on the truth. Therefore, the travails and concerns
of the world are deemed mindless by those who possess *Gnosis*.

The washing of feet is a reference to the Passover meal
and a prelude to the Eucharist, which is a symbolic reminder
of egalitarianism within the One. Here the soul is described
as strong and able to overcome the contemptible spirit. The
soul is also identified with the feminine, and can be related to
Sophia who personifies the wisdom which will lead the soul to
an eternal rest. This eternal rest is not the void of nothingness,
but a total awareness of the One, which eliminates the need for
reincarnating again and again.

Verse 9.6

*"Those who do not belong to the unshakable race will swim in forgetful-
ness. They will not awaken until they are once again thrown into the flesh.
I have now told you everything to communicate secretly to your spiritual
friends. These are the mysteries of the unshakable race."*

Those who are not part of the unshakable race will live a life of
aimless worship, and superstitious wondering. As a result, they
will have to experience reincarnation many times. They will
return to the flesh again and again, as long as they swim in the
vast ocean of meaningless seductions. However, those who are
open and awake to spiritual mysteries, are obligated to share

what they know with friends and kindred spirits, but they are not to throw spiritual wisdom before swine. For to do so can only place humanity in an even more precarious situation, and will open the gate to further persecution.

Chapter Ten

Peace Be With You... Verses 10.1-10.5

The *Gospel of Gnosis* concludes with Yeshua meeting with those whom he communes with at a common table. He does this to make it clear that he will always be with them, no matter what garment or form he takes on. We will know him by the presence of the Holy Spirit in our lives.

Verse 10.1

Those in the presence of Yeshua came to know him and love him. When reclining at table with his followers for the last time, he taught in this way, "If there is anything among my words that forms a dark cloud on the horizon, do not be worried about consulting the Christ within who is always with you."

The meal is simply the channel through which the author chooses to illustrate how important intimacy is in loving ourselves, one another, and all life eternal. For love is available to everyone, regardless of the garment they wear. Anyone who is willing to break bread with another is capable of knowing the other. Here in the breaking of bread, Yeshua teaches that he will always be with us, and any time we feel the seduction of drunkenness, or fear the approaching darkness, we only need to look within ourselves to be reminded of the healing path of *Gnosis*. For Yeshua has completed the last baptism and ascended beyond the seventh limb of the tree of life. Now, through the symbolic breaking of bread, his teaching prepares his followers for what will happen next. And if they have any doubt about the future, they only have to turn within to receive the reassurance that only comes from love eternal. This love eternal is a gift of the one God of Christ consciousness.

Verses 10.2-10.3

"Whoever loves you will love your family. Anyone in this circle embraced by the Christ can help. However, beware of those who come to devour in my name. Always put goodness as well as evil to the trial as a test for the Holy Spirit. For the resurrection is here now and always."

Love is not measured out in increments; it is unending and infinite. Therefore, true love will always love you and whomever you love. Everything is one, and therefore love cannot turn its back on itself. All comes from love and will return to the source of love. However, we must be aware of what tries to imitate love. We must even put what appears as goodness to the test, to see whether it indeed originates from the Holy Spirit, as nothing is beyond the deceptive power of pure evil. For as we pass through the baptisms and ascend the tree of life, the demiurge, who is incapable of true love, has only one jealous obsession, which is to destroy the root which leads back to the circle of trees in Paradise, which do not change, either in summer or in winter, and their leaves do not fall. For those who know them shall not taste of death.

Verse10.4

"Remember, those who are only beginning will think differently about these things. Trust in your journey, as they must trust in theirs. Follow your light given to you by the Holy Spirit and do not pay attention to the designs of the day."

We are all at different points of wakefulness on our walk through life. We must trust in our journey of direct experience, and not in that of others. For as we walk, we may think their destination is the same as ours, but it may not be so. We must therefore not judge others, or force them to walk our path. We may share a moccasin for a while, but only one person can wear one moccasin at a time. As we each follow our own path, we can only hope that our paths will cross from time to time, and that we will eventually meet under the circle of trees in Paradise which do not change.

Verse 10.5

"For those who die sober, as well as those who die drunk, will face the same God. For as the world is clothed, so will it be judged. May this be the measure of peace, so the grace of Christ may be with you always."

In the end, the garment of the body will wear out, for it is only made to house the soul for a short journey. No one can escape what awaits the soul after the body dies, whether awake or asleep, whether following the sobriety of light or the drunkenness of darkness. Each soul will return to the source from which it came. For as we chose to cloth ourselves in the world, so will we be asked to reckon ourselves with the Divine essence within. In the end, all that matters is the compassion of eternal love. So as our divine spark within is free to cross the threshold of time, may it be fully awakened as a soul filled with love.

Chapter Eleven

The Hand of the Creator... Verses 11.1-11.2

With a final embrace Yeshua makes the meaning of the gospel clear to all who have ears to hear and a clear mind to interpret the good news.

Verse 11.1

When you break bread, do so not in my memory, but rather to remember what I came to teach the world.

Here we are told that the act of breaking bread is not as important as the meaning behind it. In other words, as we gather as a faith community, we do so not to meet the impulses of the current state of affairs. Rather, we gather so the truth about creation can be ever present and evolving within us. As food is necessary to temporarily sustain a body whose destiny is death, so we must nourish the spirit with a sustenance which will never let the spirit die. Therefore, to be obsessed with the world is a hoax delivered by the god of lesser things, which ultimately results in creating the void of abandonment.

Verse 11-2

The Creator's hand is on the chosen. Therefore, strive first to be good and all else will follow. Go to the places where goodness lives. Then go to those other places and goodness will follow. This is the path which I have laid before the world, and now is the time to awaken and follow me.

To have a hand laid upon one is to be chosen from the crowd. In this way, each and every soul has been chosen to fulfill their unique purpose. The first commandment is to love God as we learn to love ourselves, and our neighbor as ourselves. As we make this our life's purpose, our love will grow to encompass not just ourselves, but to include others. This is how we put on the mantle of God's love and become the good we wish to see in the world.

Once we learn these movements of the soul, we will naturally want to share our joy and peace with others who are still searching. We will not be able to contain the luminosity of the soul. Here we become a light onto the world, which attracts other souls who are still searching. This light will manifest in the world as loving kindness; it will attract all souls. Some will not understand it, and because of their own fear and ignorance, they may attempt to extinguish it, while others may possess a more healthy curiosity, and as a result pursue the light to the ends of the Earth.

Therefore, regardless of where we go, we will attract a diversity of spiritual maturity. Hence our calling will always be to continue on our path, and to share what we know. Just as Yeshua shared with His disciples, He will continue to share with each and every one of us through the medium of Christ consciousness. In this way those who understand also know they still have much to learn. This is the path of *Gnosis,* which the Holy Spirit freely gives to all.

THE LUMINOUS WAY

$\mathcal{T}$he luminous way is the way of *Gnosis*; it is the kiss of consciousness, which awakens the soul. This kiss offers a natural, balanced, and enlightened way of being in the world without having to participate in its anxious values. The key to this relief from the world's anxieties is to continue in the way of *Gnosis*, which can come to pass through the practice of loving kindness.

Socrates once said, *"For every criticism you make of someone else, make two of yourself."* Thus every evil or ignorance we project onto others will come back to its maker in a more powerful manner. In this way, the prayer of our Lord Yeshua could be remembered not with the words, *"Forgive us our trespasses as we forgive others,"* but rather, *"Forgive me my ignorance as I forgive others their ignorance."* Focusing on sin too much is like only focusing on the symptoms of an illness and not its cause, and ultimate cure. For sin is a symptom of ignorance, which must be transformed through spiritualization. Everything we do must be done from a spiritual place, whether it is recreational, or vocational. For spirituality is the container which everything fits into; it is our vital essence which fluxes into every fiber of our being. It is the oneness which melts away all duality that separates us from the universal life force we have come to know as God.

As we experience the transformation of spiritualization, we come to know that everything already exists within the individual soul, and that this realization can only be masked by the demagogic desires of lesser things.

The *Gospel of Gnosis* introduces the reader to a new way, the luminous way. It puts the transformative process of life into words, which open the mind and soul to a new vision and its ultimate destiny of light.

The image of a tree is used because it has always been a very powerful metaphor and one we need to be awakened to. As a tree purifies the air we breathe, it also has roots which descend deep into Mother Earth. As a tree grows, it sends its roots further into the earth. As the roots spread, they are connected to one another across the entire planet. Just as electricity uses a conductor to move energy from one point to another, trees use Mother Earth as a conductor. By being grounded and aware of Mother Earth, we become grounded and rooted to one another. This is the knowledge that all spiritual work is energy work. As the lower soul begins its liberation and ascent to the realm of the higher soul, it will explore and experience many manifestations of energy. This rising is the journey of the soul as it is attracted to the emanations of the one true life force of Creation.

This rising can be likened to how both trees and people begin life as a seed which then grows limbs. Each limb has its purpose and, as it grows older, it can support more life. As we grow, we must learn to adapt to life. The five baptisms give us a metaphor for evolving as spiritual beings. Figure 1 on the opposite page illustrates the procession of the five baptisms.

As we recognize sin as a symptom of ignorance, we come to understand both forethought and afterthought as a loving God bringing awareness into our consciousness. Anyone who is unable to see themselves as one with God only has to bring the divine within before their consciousness. At once they will see

The Baptisms	The Seeker	Growth Stages	Levels of Guidance
Enrobing ritual crossing over	asks for *Gnosis*	Beguiled Mysticism	The Catechumen
Washing conversion proselyte	receives *Gnosis*	Emotional Defilement	The Neophyte
Glorifying novice	lives *Gnosis*	Noetic Concentration	The Disciple
Enthroning apprentice ascetic	shares *Gnosis*	Transcendent Discipline	The Gnostic
Luminosity awakened enlightened	carries *Gnosis*	Tutelary renewal	The Elder

Figure 1
The Five Baptisms

themselves elevated to a better and more authentic beauty. To be one with God is to be one with all of nature, for the purpose of nature is to elevate the person. To be ignorant of nature is to be ignorant of God, and to defile oneself and the One. Today we are all witnesses to the defilement of Mother Earth and will one day all be accountable to her.

Here we must remember that evil desires impact on consciousness more violently than desires which are more agreeable and pleasant. A desire for evil will always leave one with less knowledge of the wisdom of Sophia. The residue of shock and ugliness will cause the soul much sickness and produce much damage to the garment of the body. For example, we all have seen people whose bodies have aged prematurely, because they have wantonly abused them. On the other hand, Sophia herself can leave the soul and the garment of the body immersed in a healthy tranquility. This is a natural process which the soul desires, unlike the unnatural process which produces conditions for sickness which spread like a spiritual cancer in the soul.

For the soul to find the strength to see its own divinity within it must follow the stages of growth, which is a natural progression from duality to becoming unified with the One.

The problems of today are global problems. We are no longer relegated to tribes or suffer the restrictions of feudalism. Although colonialism is a generational abuse, which still has its grasp on many societies, globalization has given rise to global issues of the soul. Once again, we only have to refer to addiction, which is simply a form of greed, to see how its global influence has been destroying Mother Earth's natural resources. We only have to look at our use of fossil fuels to see how our global addiction to oil has quickly eroded the moral fabric of humanity. The abuse we are subjecting the planet to is close to becoming equal to mass suicide. This is a chilling pattern of addiction and the most insane example of how psychological trends are enabling greed to commit the atrocities of environmental madness. Why does society tolerate this mass suicidal ideation? Is there any greater madness than ignoring a runaway train that is causing irreversible damage to the planet, and maybe also the solar system, which is already littered with space junk?

As addiction grows, we continue to respond to its impact on civilization with antiquated business models that are also based on greed. The old treatment models are not working, because those who have designed them have lost their souls, and have created an enterprise of greed. Greed or addiction has become a commodity which is eating away at the root of the tree of life.

What is at stake has become unparalleled and grievous for all humanity. To deal with humanity's insatiable greed we need to remove the focus from global narcissistic dependencies, and focus more on the disastrous effects that oppressive global co-dependencies exert on society at large. For example, we need to provide treatment for addiction that offers alternatives to greedy lifestyles. In this way all the greed and evil in the world will run out of places to hide. They can be backed into a corner where choices based on spiritual realities can be made. However, this is the last stand, which will be met with much resistance on the part of greed. The only way to successfully combat this greed is to do so with loving kindness. When this happens, humanity will have no option but to turn back to *Gnosis* for its survival. This is the only way the destructive path humanity is on can be altered, and the devastation it is leaving in its wake can be reduced. This is the final option which exists in the heart of the soul.

To put it simply, the injustices and dependencies of greed need to be treated. Society has become so pathologically reliant upon and fixated with greed, it has lost almost all ability to rationally deal with the internal blindness of the lower soul. This part of the soul therefore feels lost, confused and apathetic. Its eternal sleep is created by the seductive trance of greed, and is in desperate need of the kiss of consciousness to wake it up. In human terms, we can no longer ignore the fact that all humanity is on the same sinking ship. Once those being pulled under by a drowning greedy society break free from this addicted lifestyle, the seductive dance of trance can finally be cast off.

From the perspective of the higher soul, which is always free of trance and materialism, the lower soul must be willing to enter the dark night and feel its own pain. When this happens, the lower soul will become liberated and aware of how it is responsible for creating its own pain. Then healthy self-care based on loving kindness becomes a powerful means of intervention. This premise also applies to individual families, just as it does to the global family. In other words, we must continue to care for the obsessed individual. However, we must also remember to support the caregiver. This is a very difficult task, because we have all been conditioned for centuries to be martyrs. Once we begin to understand that martyrdom is a deception created by greed to keep others enslaved, then all humanity can begin to experience the collective liberty of *Gnosis*.

Mother Earth has always been able to provide for all our needs. There will always be enough for everyone, if we learn how to share the work as well as the gifts. The competitive monetary systems we have developed are not written in stone, and are based on greed. Resource systems based on cooperation, and sharing communities are actually more productive and more virtuous in inspiring the quest for the common good. Therefore, development of a resource based system, motivated by loving kindness, is the obvious next step in our biological, psychological, and spiritual evolution. The tree of life is a symbol of abundance, which awakened systems of *Gnosis* are founded on. The more capable we become in acquiring *Gnosis,* the more efficient we will become in distributing prosperity fairly.

By pursuing self-love we can more easily love our neighbor and avoid the deceptions of martyrdom. For to love the self is to love God and our neighbor as ourselves. When we are willing to evolve through *Gnosis*, we can learn to direct our energies toward the common good. When we do, we will be gaining entry to the kingdom of heaven. The *Gospel of Gnosis* tells us, *"The kingdom of heaven is with us always, but those occupied by the world do not see it."* To love the self and avoid martyrdom is the way of *Gnosis*, and the way to discover the natural and common good, which all life aspires to.

The face of God may be compared to the wind. It is invisible, but is present everywhere. And like the wind, the Creator who is everywhere would not have created the world without offering the soul a way to exist in it in peace and happiness. The *Gospel of Gnosis* helps us focus on why we are here, and how we should live in the created world, while we are still in the body. This will give us enough to ponder to last many lifetimes.

So let us now ponder the words of Plotinus, as he beautifully describes the soul being released from the garment of the body:

And if you do not find yourself beautiful yet, act as does a creator of a statue that is to be made beautiful: he cuts away here, he smooths there, he makes this line lighter, this other purer, until a lovely face has grown upon his work. So do you also cut away all that is excessive, straighten all that is crooked, bring light to all that is overcast, labor to make all one glow of beauty and never cease chiseling your statue, until there shall shine out on you from it the godlike splendor of virtue, until you shall see the perfect goodness surely established in the stainless shrine?

When you know that you have become this perfect work, when you are self-gathered in the purity of your being, nothing now remaining that can shatter that inner unity, nothing from without clinging to the authentic man, when you find yourself wholly true to your essential nature, wholly that only veritable Light which is not measured by space, not narrowed to any circumscribed form... ever unmeasurable as something greater than all measure and more than all quantity—when you perceive that you have grown to this, you are now become vision itself; now call up all your confidence, strike forward yet a step—you need a guide no longer—strain and see.

Plotinus Ennead I.6.9

We know that literalism thinks inside the box and that liberalism thinks outside the box. But only a renewal of the human spirit through *Gnosis* has no box to contend with. For the One has shown us over and over again that only humility is the rightful heir of knowledge and intelligence. For when one forsakes humility, one merely becomes civilized and finds sophisticated ways to hide one's arrogance, greed and ignorance. Therefore, now is a good time, in fact the only time, to ponder the spiritual realities of the one within the One.

THE COSMIC SOLUTION

I searched for God and found only myself.
I searched for myself and found only God.

Sufi Proverb

Gnosis is the gift of the cosmos. It is the cosmic response to an awakened consciousness. In the true fashion of *Gnosis*, I cannot tell you how to interpret these words; you must find the meaning within yourself. However, I can share with you what finding the cosmic solution means to me.

We often hear *Gnosis* described as secret knowledge by those who do not understand it. This is the first falsehood we must correct—*Gnosis* is not a secret. It is free and available to everyone. Some search for it, and others do not, but every living creature in the cosmos has the potential to develop it. The only requirement is the desire to do so. Creatures that exist by instinct do this naturally and as a result they live in harmony within creation. We see this very clearly in the evolution of nature. Creatures like humans, who have evolved to embody mindfulness, must contend with ego. As a result, humans must also contend with the awareness, or lack of awareness of their state of being. This is where *Gnosis* can cause confusion, for it can mean different things to different people, while others might not even give it a second thought.

For instance, let's make a simple comparison. Some people, who self-identify as *gnostic*, would say that the soul is trapped in the body, and while in this earthy domain it spends its time waiting to be released. Fair enough. But let's use a different narrative to make a comparison. If I were to be asked to get into a car with a person I knew was incapable of driving, my higher sensibilities would say no. If I did not pay attention to my higher self, and got into the car, I might be trapped in the car as the vehicle became driven recklessly. However, if I had listened to my intuitive inner voice, which was saying not to get into the car, then I would have chosen the better path. This does not mean that when I am driving in my own car, and follow all the rules of the road, I still cannot experience an accident caused by another driver on the freeway of life who is navigating carelessly.

What this little thought experiment tells us is that if we see the soul as trapped, we will be creating for it a life of conflict. If, on the other hand, we view the soul as co-existing with the body, we will be able to co-exist with our soul in harmony. It all depends on the choices we make, as the higher consciousness of the soul speaks to us. Sometimes we choose to listen to our higher consciousness, which we all have the opportunity to develop, and at other times we ignore it to our own detriment. As a result, we can experience frustration, depression, anger, and all the so-called negative emotions. This is the domain of the lower self, while the emotions of joy, peace, and harmony are the domain of the higher self.

You only have to look at the short time human beings have been on the planet to see how we have evolved. First, we evolved through a primitive life force. Secondly, we evolved through a primordial life force. Thirdly, we evolved through a magical life force. Fourthly, we evolved through a mythical life force. All four of these levels of consciousness have been experienced by humanity on a collective level. Some have progressed slowly, while others have progressed quickly. Those who developed quickly became the spiritual leaders of the world. Unfortunately, they are in the minority. However, as human beings continue to evolve, we can spiritualize exponentially.

This evolution of spirit is the evolution of human consciousness. This next stage in the cosmic solution will provide humanity with all the solutions to human conflict. For instance, I cannot be in another person's body. Therefore, my soul can only live in my own body. Our earlier car example demonstrates how we can join others in their car as a passenger, but if we do, we will be driven to the destination they are committed to. The only way we can arrive at our own true destination is to be driving our own car. In some cases we may share a path and, as a result, we may be comfortable being on the same bus as others who share our path. But only one person can drive the bus at a time. So the question now becomes, who is driving the bus? Or who's life are you living?

Let's take a closer look at the four life forces, which have brought humanity to the next stage of our evolution, also known as the cosmic solution.

The Primitive Life Force

The primitive life force reflects the old brain function of humanity. This is the reptilian brain which is governed by our fight, flight, or freeze survival mechanisms. This part of the brain connects to the spinal cord. The brain stem controls the functions which are fundamental to the survival of all animals, such as heart rate, breathing, digesting foods, and sleeping. It is the lowest, most primitive area of the human brain.

The Primordial Life Force

The primordial life force is the seat of such emotions as thirst, hunger, and pain. It also controls the feelings which guide us in our decision making process. These feelings have given humans the ability to become self-aware; they are the foundations of a personal identity. This reflective consciousness has emerged as a result of the development of cognition.

The Magical Life Force

The magical life force is attributed to synchronistic relationships, actions and events which seemingly cannot be justified by reason and observation. Thus religion and superstition are correlated with religious ritual, prayer, sacrifice, and with the expectation of a benefit or reward. Believing in a magical life force can cause a person to experience performance anxieties, or lead them to assume their actions have special powers. In doing so, they may become a danger to themselves and others. As a result they block the reception of purer levels of consciousness. Magical thinking can lead people to believe that their thoughts or actions can bring about the desired effects in the world. Due to synchronicity, their actions are misinterpreted and can fuel the reasoned fallacies of groups and cults.

The Mythical Life Force

Myths are usually based on a modicum of truth. Then they quickly become falsehoods that are widely believed. Once a perception of truth is established, myths can be disguised in the science of the day, which is easily passed on without question Anecdotally, myth has its place; it creates a playground in the imagination, and gives potential to the mysteries of reality yet to be discovered. But it takes courage to challenge the legitimacy of a myth cloaked in pseudoscience. Myths about consciousness are gaining widespread traction because of our limited understanding of the mind.

The Cosmic Life Force

To make some sense of all this, let's draw a very simplified and brief timeline of the evolution of human consciousness.

Firstly, we evolved as *homo sapiens* through a primitive world view, complete with cave paintings that point to the existence of a soul.

Secondly, we developed primordial functions of our thoughts connected to feelings. We now evolved not only as thinkers, but as feelers.

Thirdly, our magical thinking developed due to our growing self-awareness, which introduced us to an ego identity.

Fourthly, after thousands of years of human evolution on a planet that has taken millions of years to be prepared for our arrival, we search for meaning by establishing myths to guide us.

Now that we have evolved to this point, humanity must continue its evolution by abandoning outdated archetypes. However, not everyone is ready to move on. Yet, those who must move on do so because the soul is always seeking harmony, not conflict. There will be resistance. This is normal as part of the process. So before we discuss the cosmic life force, let us look at how those of us who are ready to move on can help those who are still seeking. Let us take a moment to reflect on the narrative of body memories to make sense of the limits of the intellect.

Body Awareness

The Creator made a material world, and wanted us to enjoy it. So we were given a soul to live in while existing in the material world. The Creator wanted us to be happy in this body, but evolution has its challenges. As a result, the soul, which has difficulty befriending the body, may feel trapped. It can also enjoy its time in the body, and feel joy and happiness. For instance, some souls reject their primitive urges to seek pleasure in the body, and construct magical thoughts and myths about the flesh. Religion has been a major player in the soul's avoidance of being human. Even to this day, many people have a problem providing children with a truthful and healthy introduction to the body. Here we can once again use the analogy of a car. Many people only see the body as a vehicle to get around. We have lost contact with the body. We use it like many other useful material things; we have forgotten how to breathe, walk, smell, taste, hear, see, and touch. No wonder that some souls feel trapped. Our bodies have been conditioned by the spiritually immature to shun what gives us pleasure in the flesh. Once we can overcome this harmful view of life, we will no longer feel like a soul trapped in the prison of a body; we will feel like a soul in harmony with the body, existing in a material world given to us by the Creator. This is an important awareness, if we want to live in a material world that supports peace and harmony. Such a world would become a safe and friendly place, where our time in the body is limited, as we prepare for cosmic unity.

Emotional Awareness

Next, we need to pay more attention to our feelings and emotions. After all, if we cannot feel emotion, how can we show compassion to ourselves and others? In a patriarchal society emotional intelligence has become weakened. For our consciousness to evolve, it is paramount for humanity to wake up to our emotions. We must learn to balance our masculine and feminine energies; we need to become more aware of our integrated sexuality. In today's world we are hearing more and more about transgenderism. If we really think about this, does it not make sense that God is transgendered—both male and female? If we become open to Goddess energy, we will be shown the way back to the Oneness of Creation.

Natural Awareness
It does not take much to see how humanity has lost its way in terms of its connection to Mother Earth. We have progressed from the Garden of Eden to the destruction of the planet by climate change. An evolved consciousness would not let these things happen. Instead, we have perpetuated further myths, such as, "Technology will find answers to solve the threat of climate change," or, "We will one day be able to colonize the moon or Mars for the survival of humanity." The biggest myth or falsehood is that climate change does not exist. An evolved consciousness would not commit suicide! An evolved consciousness would foster a world shift that could eliminate the economics of greed. It is no wonder that some of the most impoverished peoples living in developed countries are their indigenous peoples. They have become the voice of Mother Earth. And let's face it, until Mother Earth has breathed her last breath, she will continue to be raped by the unconscious commerce of greed.

Personal Awareness
We did not enter the material world to be perfect; we came to be human, to develop consciousness on the material plain. To do this we only need to remember. For we do not discover or

invent anything; we only remember what has always been there, waiting for us to discover. As we progress in consciousness, we will also progress in prayer and meditation. This is the chicken and egg problem: which comes first? Do we pray and meditate to discover consciousness, or does consciousness cause us to pray and meditate? The answer is that probably both are true. This is why mindfulness and *Gnosis* are making such a resurgence. Humanity is on the cusp of remembering, and as it begins to remember, the old myths, dogmas, and archetypes will be replaced, but not forgotten. For to forget our shared history is a mistake doomed to repeat itself. We will remember our ancestors as we stand on their shoulders. The journey is personal, and we will begin to remember more and more with every cell of our body, mind, and soul. This will help us remember what existed even before the chicken or the egg. It is remembering what existed prior to the big bang and pre-space—the first emanations of the One.

Interpersonal Awareness

Consciousness is an awakening force. As consciousness awakens us further, it will let us remember our personal journey within a body, with a mind and soul. Once we remember, we will be able to connect with others on an interpersonal level. This is a place to talk, listen, commune, and engage with one another with compassion and joy. As this happens to individuals, they will be overcome with hope, and will want to reach out to others to share their joy. The others will be experienced as a reflection of the individual, and will become a life force of the people, by the people, for the people.

Transpersonal Awareness

As we communicate and draw strength from one another, we

will also clearly hear the call of nature. We will listen to all life. The birds, the water, the trees, the mountains, and the entire cosmos will not only be heard, but understood. Our oneness will be understood, and humanity will be catapulted into a new world order destined for the next level of eternity.

The Cosmic Solution

The cosmic solution is embodied in the cross, but not the Christian cross—just a universal, or cosmic cross symbolizing the intersection of divine consciousness and human evolution. As we learn to mature and spiritualize, we will experience all emotions beyond what we have experienced to this point in our human evolution—emotions that we have never felt before, as our minds, hearts, and souls open to a new consciousness. Human beings will be known as *homo spiritualis,* en route to a new communion with and in the One. The cosmos is a universe seen as a well-ordered system of thought. So here is a thought experiment: if humans have DNA, is it not logical that God also has DNA? Therefore, why couldn't the cosmos possess DNA? Any visit to a planetarium or astronomical reserve will no doubt remind the soul of how vast the cosmos is. This awe-inspiring experience is the soul trying to remember; it can trigger a longing in the soul to look deeply within. And in the depth of the soul we will discover its endless beauty and diversity; we will come to know that each of us is an individual thought of God. And in knowing this we will renew our inner search for *Gnosis.* For if we are all individual thoughts of God, then there is nothing new to discover; we only need to remember anew, and with new eyes see the world and the cosmos as co-creators. Just imagine—everything that will ever exist already exists. And everything that exists can be shaped anew. Here we are back to the chicken and the egg concept of limited awareness.

The cosmic solution rests in the age-old human question —what is my purpose and the meaning of my life and all life? Where have I been, where am I now, and where am I going next? The cosmic solution is consciousness evolving to the next ultimate level, followed by the next, and the next. Forget about getting to the moon or Mars on a spaceship; we will arrive there much sooner by an evolved consciousness and awareness of the One.

In talking with an aboriginal elder from South America, I was shown in a very real and concrete way how to space travel, not as an astronaut, but by becoming an "innernaut." This may sound crazy to many, but not to anyone with even a tiny amount of cosmic awareness. For those who want to continue to evolve on this human journey, we can leave this world without having to leave the body or planet Earth. All we have to do is have the desire and the universe will provide the cosmic solution.

Back to the Cosmic Solution

The world we live in is vast and boundless. The human race may be confined to live in a small portion of the world, but people are aware of the existence of other planets and galaxies within the cosmos.

The word cosmos comes from the Greek word *kosmos*, which means order or orderly. The cosmos is a whole harmonious and orderly system that is governed by natural laws. To recognize that we are part of something much larger than ourselves can usher in openness to the cosmic solution.

The cosmic solution is the human embodiment of a mindful loving kindness. It is the flowering of the best humanity has to offer as our contribution to making the world become a better place. For only God knows what lies beyond our small planet Earth. *Gnosis* has always been a gift, which has been left unopened for too long. It is the path of awakening, which can lead us across the threshold to a new super-consciousness.

An important attribute of energy is that it transforms and that this transformational energy is perpetual. Therefore a person may surmise that their consciousness is preserved after they depart this earthly life. In every corner of the cosmos energy and life co-exist. One of these is immortal in origin and waits beyond humankind. The cosmos is purely spiritual and is therefore more harmonious and moral than humanity.

A lack of human awareness leads to a lack of human morality and harmony, which causes great cosmic pain. Therefore, the depth of suffering exists as a malady which the majority of humans are not even aware of. As a result misery, evil, wars, and other forms of suffering become meaningless and bring about a horrifying condition of ignorance.

Only once these truths are accepted will humanity come to realize that we are connected body, mind, emotions and soul. Once the power of *Gnosis* is revealed and embraced, humanity will come to know that we are connected by invisible strands of love!

Let us ponder a new way of being, so we may individually and collectively transcend, not only the limits of a soul within the body, but transcend the collective soul of the Earth, as it becomes part of the cosmos and its cosmic solution. We have heaven on Earth. Let us open our eyes through *Gnosis* to see it both in the here and the hereafter. For as souls we can expand with the universe, as part of the heavenly realm of God.

A Gnostic Psalm

Let us worship the Holy Spirit who has sent us the spirit of truth.
For it came and separated us from the error of the world.
It brought us a mirror.
We looked into it and saw in it the universe.

REBIRTH

$\mathcal{I}$t is a risky business to cut ourselves off from all forms of religion. To do so means we will be in danger of abandoning part of our authentic selves in the process. This opens the door even wider for the habits of our shadow nature to cause chaos in our lives and the lives of others. We must always remember that our essence is divine and, as a result, the divine can never turn its back on us, because in doing so it would be turning its back on itself. Religion is a human expression, and when ignored, it can become the playground of the shadow. We should not be tempted to abandon religion, in the sense that if we do, we will be cutting ourselves off from one another and ourselves. No matter how much we try to eliminate religion from our lives, it will never go away. Let us therefore follow the cosmic solution given to the soul through *Gnosis*, to reclaim the God- given beauty of religion.

In doing so may all human inventions of religion be born anew through an elevated and natural divine consciousness. Within the mind of God there is room for a new unifying universal religion. This new religion may be just as multiple and varied as there are people—past, present, and future. If humanity hopes to survive the dark denials of the collective future that awaits us, we all need to wake up soon. If not now, then when will it be the right time for human beings on this glorious planet to wake up to the diversity and depth of our ignorance? The time is now for a new reformation of the soul, progressing from organized religion to a seemingly unorganized religion of the people of Mother Earth. This will no doubt be scary for many, especially the organized religions. But religion is just a means and not the end. The end is awareness of the divinization of Mother Earth, and survival of the planet for future generations to continue the dream of cosmic spiritualization.

It is said that humility is the rightful heir of knowledge and intelligence. Understanding this can help us cross the threshold where the material world and consciousness meet. For example, let us look at the centuries-old practice of walking a labyrinth, which is a walking meditation. It is a way to move the materiality of the physical body, as we invoke the spirituality of consciousness. We begin by standing at the threshold of the labyrinth, full of intention. As we cross the threshold, we begin walking down a threefold path. The first path of purging is experienced as we move to the center of the labyrinth. The second path of receiving is the awareness we experience as we spend time at the center of the labyrinth. The third path of union we experience as we make our way out of the labyrinth. Finally, once again we pass the same threshold. However, this time, as we return to the material world, we do so with a new conscious awareness.

The labyrinth is a very powerful grace which has been known for centuries. Today we drive and fly everywhere, while creating an environmental footprint. However, there was a time when walking was the main mode of transportation and the only footprints we would leave were the indentations made by our feet in the sand. Just imagine the Buddha or Jesus walking from town to town—there was no other way to get around, except maybe on the back of an animal, or in a cart that was being pulled by an animal that would also be walking. This was much slower than a car or plane, and afforded the pilgrim a lot of time to think mindfully. In fact, at the time the historical Jesus walked the Earth, some Greek decorative patterns on the Corinthian pillars resembled the pattern of a labyrinth. One could therefore hypothesize that Jesus may have walked a labyrinth. Of course, there is no evidence of this happening, but it is a curious thought.

Today I can drive or fly anywhere in the world while covering great distances. But the question remains—how mindful am I when I am sitting in a cozy seat, focused on the latest tablet or business endeavor? We may think we are being mindful or constructive, but this is once again another beguilement. For the technologies of today only provide the illusion of free time, when in reality they only provide us with more time to do more things. Our ancestors had no inflight movies, computers, tablets, or phones to cause distraction. They were predisposed to be alone with themselves and the Creator. This is how a labyrinth works—it prompts us to be mindful and slowly develop a deeper consciousness. However, we have to make a personal choice to do so. And let's face it, how mindful can you be when you are being unknowingly beguiled?

The idea here is not to ignore technology, but to technologically move forward, guided by the enlightened principles of *Gnosis*. The crisis humanity faces today is not just environmental; it is much bigger than that. The biggest crisis we face today is evolutionary. It is only though the development of a higher consciousness that the human race can learn to survive the man-made tragedies like war, famine, and heartache. The dark night does not have to linger, once the lessons of an evolved consciousness are sought and embraced through the grace of *Gnosis*. The dark night does not have to spell a violent end to the human race. The great hope is that humanity will accept rebirth, as the soul finds its way back to its original state of perfection, reborn as a holy child of Christ consciousness. For there are no limits to be placed on the boundaries of consciousness.

A boundless consciousness transcends the cranial brain, and must include the brain that we refer to as our gut. This abdominal brain, which is connected to the cranial brain, is what helps us remain in balance and harmony. Like yin and yang, or the feminine and masculine principles, consciousness becomes a grounding force, when experienced from a place of sublime openness. To be mindful is a function of the cranial brain—for instance, being mindful of my breath, or the sensation of my bare feet on the ground. Wakefulness, on the other hand, is a function of the abdominal brain—to be awake to the truthfulness of an intuitive state of mind. When these two conditions are harmonious with each other, the door to super-consciousness can be opened. Therefore, for our consciousness to evolve, we must be both mindful and wakeful; we must utilize both our cranial and abdominal brains. In doing so, the current of energy between chakras will flow more openly. From this place of openness we will begin to see that the mind is not located in the brain. In fact, we will begin to understand that the mind is not centered within us at all. Rather, we are centered in the mind. As previously shared, we can all be unravelled as individual thoughts embraced by a loving Creator. This new paradigm will shift our thinking from an egocentric world view to a more integrated and unified world view. This more evolved world view is the path which leads to our connection with the savior of humankind.

To establish this paradigm firmly in our awakened state, we need only turn to the greatest disease of our time. Some would suggest cancer, depression, or a host of other maladies could pass for the worst of the worst, but these are only symptoms of old ailments. The name for the ailment, which has been with humanity since the beginning of time, is loneliness. Today loneliness is the disease of the unloved and unwanted. Our modern solution to loneliness is short-sighted and technical in nature. Alcohol, drugs, or the latest fad, or gadget create new seductions, which only perpetuate the problem. This leads to the birthing of scarcity, which is the companion of greed.

Loneliness kills. It is a disease of the soul. Loneliness is fueled by isolation and traps the mind in the body, attempting to kill the spirit, and dim the light within. Loneliness kills people and relationships by war and starvation. I have known people who have died from a broken heart. The cranial brain may attribute death of the physical body to cancer, suicide, or addiction, but to the intuitive abdominal brain, the cause of these people's spirits to leave the body is loneliness.

The solution to loneliness is cosmic; it can only come from the marriage of both the cranial and abdominal brain, the yin and yang—a complete union of the feminine and the masculine found in Christ consciousness.

As you read the pages of the *Gospel of Gnosis*, you can find every solution to every human problem. This sounds implausible. But truthfully, are not the real answers to life's conflicts simple? Solutions are always nestled next to peace, forgiveness, gratitude, charity, faith, hope, and love. The difficultly is always caused by denial and implementation. It is our human need for drama, guided by inflated egos, which directs us down pathways of destruction. The solutions to human problems will always come from evolved consciousness, not the next gadget. However, not many people want to do the personal work to get there. The seduction of a softer and easier way is very enticing. Just imagine that all the human tribulations you have ever experienced can be repaired and reconciled by working on your personal evolution as a human being. In the beginning, the answers to your difficulties will not seem obvious, but they are there. You only have to search the heart with the intention of seeking conscious wholeness, then the cosmic solution will appear.

Wakefulness is always waiting for us at the threshold of consciousness to invite us in. The more I breathe and live mindfully, the more I will be awakened to the seduction of non-entities, which enter our world as the next shiny thing. The ignorance of humanity is damming for all life on planet Earth, but it can also be seen as the key which turns the lock to a deeper consciousness, to be discovered beyond the threshold of ignorance. The gatekeeper to humanity's next evolution is ignorance, for what is rooted can easily be nourished. This is another way of saying that the squeaky wheel gets the oil. In humanity's case, this can be taken quite literally. For we now live in a society which worships the golden calf.

We must remember that the soul wants more, because it has been designed by the Creator to grow and evolve. But if it is fooled into following the needs of non-entities, it will evolve only in the realm of the lower self. This is why when we feel depressed, or sad, we ask ourselves, "Is this all there is to life?" And the answer for those seeking a higher existence is always, "No." This is when the ignorance of the soul dissipates in the pursuit of spiritualization.

Gnosis itself is not hidden within the pages of the *Gospel of Gnosis*. However, these pages do arouse something deep within our shared human reality that is waiting to be set free. By contrast, as individuals and societies become obsessed with a beguiled mysticism, it will give birth to something unique within the individual. Something dark and foreboding has been given life. Likewise, when the individual or society refuses to invite beguilement into its life, they will be free to attract a truth, which will give birth to something unique and hopeful within. This something will shed light on the darkness and open the mind, body and soul to the universal truth called *Gnosis*. This universal truth is the awareness hidden deep within, as you experience the mysterious spiritual realities of your cosmic self being born anew with super Christ consciousness.

FUTURE PERSPECTIVES

Measuring the Evolution of Consciousness

As we lean into the future, what will be the demands on consciousness? What challenges and gifts will we be offered as we evolve as a species? Since evolution normally happens slowly, how will we recognize progress? One marker we can use to measure our evolving consciousness is the empty pew.

The Empty Pew

The evidence is clear: many religious institutions are becoming less attended and the pews are empty. As the human race evolves more and more, people will wake up in greater numbers. As people wake up, the days of a cleric preaching to a congregation will be over. People have no time to listen to shameless sermons that are lectures devoid of any practical relevance. This is because individuals are developing the capacity to draw from their own direct experience of the divine. The empty pew can therefore be seen as a positive indicator that humanity is evolving, and finally breaking free of the chains of organized religion. However, since we all evolve individually, and at our own pace, there will always be many who still prefer to participate in outdated religious observances. Sheeple never want to stray from the steeple. As a result, they contribute to their own demise by participating in the colonization of their minds. Once people stop believing in the economic myths created by those who would contribute to the colonization of minds, they can begin to live a more sustainable and peaceful lifestyle. So, in retrospect, the empty pew refers to the liberation from the thought reforms initiated by any religious institution which is invested in continuously feeding sheeple the slop of outdated dogmas.

From Pulpit to Pew

Today artificial intelligence and emotional intelligence have been woven together, but each still exists in its own independent state. There are many well-intentioned individuals who promote the benefits of civic virtues, and are advocates of the hypothesis that one day computers will possess consciousness. But this is just another beguilement, produced at the hands of economic colonization. For example, now that corporations enjoy the legal status of personhood, they are hoping to further colonize the minds of humanity by declaring that they are not only human, but that they possess consciousness. This, of course, is only smoke and mirrors, and there is no science behind any of the hype about artificial intelligence developing consciousness. There are those people who believe that at some point in the distant future science will be able to copy a brain that possesses consciousness, but there is absolutely no evidence that this will ever be possible.

From Pew to Pulpit

With the awakening of consciousness, people will no longer be dependent on gurus. Direct spiritual experience eliminates the middle man, known as religion. This will impact greatly on the future of religion. In fact, we can already see the conflict between pulpit and pew happening. The people in the pulpit will have to listen to the people in the pew, if they want to remain viable and relevant. Religion will still have its place as a social construct, but its ability to be a unifying force will be with the people. What has just been described could just as easily evolve into another guru or religion becoming the next *tour de force*. However, once the number of people waking up to pure levels of consciousness passes a tipping point, the future of religion as a collective social construct can also change. It will finally be led by the enlightened hearts of the people of *Gnosis*.

The Gift of Pleasure and Pain

The human condition is hard wired to respond to both pleasure and pain. If we like something, we want more; and if we don't like something, we try to avoid it. However, the simple paradox is that sometimes what is best for us is pain, and what is not good for us is pleasure. The following quote from a transformed hedonist illustrates this point, as they state, *"If it feels good, then don't do it, and if it does not feel good, then do that instead."* It seems humanity has always taken the hard road, which is well travelled. But in this example we can find the key which can open the door to a more evolved consciousness. For what is pain or pleasure, other than the same root of energy vibrating at different ends of the spectrum?

As humans, we are complex, and we will always face one dilemma after another. This is the continuum of life as a saint or a sinner. It is both the curse and the grace of being an embodied spiritual being. The challenge is to correctly discern what is right for us as individuals and trust in the process of our transcendent virtues. For instance, just try practicing the law of opposites. When angry, practice love, or when afraid, practice courage. These are emotions from both ends of the spectrum. As such, they are connected to one another. As we grow in consciousness, we will also grow in the higher vibrations of love, rather than the lower vibrations of hate. Since all our emotions are connected, they will also intersect with all the other emotions within our spiritual repertoire. Just imagine what it will be like to discover new feelings and spiritual experiences we had never known before.

If we devote all our faculties towards the development of self-knowledge, we will discover such noble gifts of being and growth by which all humankind may be perfected. As we grow in self-awareness, we will nurture a consciousness that actively acquires good habits and conquers our bad habits. Anyone who is ignorant of their own spiritual potential is dangerously close to the denial of all spiritual reality.

In the *Gospel of Luke*, Martha and Mary choose to use their time with Jesus in different ways. Martha begins to work and prepare a place for Jesus, while Mary simply sits with him and waits. As a result Jesus says, *"Mary has chosen the better way."* Mary has chosen to enter her hidden heart and look deeply into her unknown self. Here she will learn the secrets of her existence. For in eternity there is no need for works of mercy, as we see them now. God is calling all humanity to enter into the fog of eternity, as consciousness is realized within each and every one of us. And as each person matures spiritually, they will abound more and more in the energies of love. For the soul who answers the call of *Gnosis* will receive the eternal heavenly rewards of super Christ consciousness. And when the time comes to leave a lasting footprint on Mother Earth, it will be cast as a loving presence for all to remember.

Acquired knowledge can only bring us to the threshold of spiritual experience. To truly experience God, we must cross the threshold of knowing and enter the ineffable dwelling where we alone can reside in the presence of God. For it is only at the table of the One that we can truly enjoy all the spiritual delights the eternal kingdom has to offer.

As we gaze into the future, what is being reflected back to humanity is an age of dataism, and computers. As we cross this new threshold into the future, are we becoming more robotic, or more human? What is this doing to human resilience? There is an old adage which states, "You must eat a peck of dirt to be healthy." We know that as we learn to live a more sterile existence, the ability for our immune systems to fight illness is beginning to malfunction. The same can be said about our psyches. As our minds become more robotic through years of colonialism, thought reform, and conditioning, this old adage still remains true. In other words, our psyches must eat a peck of dirt to remain healthy. This is how we remain resilient, free thinkers. We must experience all the emotions available for the human condition to thrive. This is where Mary's world view differs from Martha's. Mary had chosen the better way because she was open to what the human experience had to offer. Martha had chosen the lesser way, and by denying her emotional life, she fell prey to the seduction of vain promises. To be human means we must learn to mature spiritually by loving all life, including the parts which repulse us. We all have warts and secrets we keep from one another, but these secrets are only an illusion, once we understand that nothing can be hidden from the Creator, and therefore nothing can be hidden from us. We may think we can hide by investing our emotional life in the seductions of the world, but we must always remember that mammon makes a better slave than a master.

Let us end with a brief thought experiment. Picture something in your mind which generates feelings of consolation—your children, husband, wife, or a puppy. What does this image stir inside you? Now think of a stranger whom you have never met, who lives on the other side of the planet. What does this stir inside you? Probably not very much. Now think about a time when these feelings of consolation had to be projected onto another person through compassion—maybe your partner or that adorable puppy. Next, try to project those same feelings onto someone you don't know, or even like. Maybe you see an angry person scolding a puppy. How does this make you feel about that person? How do you feel about the puppy? The ability to feel compassion varies in all of these instances. Our ability to love may have a low range. Just like a car with a half empty tank of gas will have a shorter range than the same car with a full tank of gas, so, too, does the vehicle of the soul have a smaller ability to feel compassion when it is low on the fuel of God's love. The point here is that God's tank is always full. As a result, it is easier to love ourselves and feel compassion for those close to us than for those further away. However, God loves every form of life on the planet equally, completely, and unconditionally. For how else can balance and harmony be maintained?

Just imagine that the way you love yourself, or feel sadness and compassion for yourself, is also the way God actually feels about every person on the planet. This tells me that in my lower human nature I cannot be a divine expression of God, but in my higher divine nature I can share in God's love and compassion. Is it not a comfort to know that God loves every person on the planet more than I can possibly love myself? This is something to remember the next time you are walking down a busy street, or sitting in a shopping mall people watching.

Every person has someone who loves them in this world or the next. We are all born of a divine source of love, which was present in our mother's womb. We all therefore receive the gift of love at birth, as our soul enters the physical body. Therefore, as we judge another who is angry, challenged, or joyful, we must always do our best to be mindful that they are loved and created like us, to love and be loved, even if the only love left in their life comes from God. We must do our best to always remember that we are all loved by the Creator, and as part of creation we have a spiritual calling to participate in making the cosmos a beautiful and welcoming place. For as we watch others, so, too, is God watching over us. God is the power that connects us to one another and keeps our tank full. *"So as the world is clothed, so will it be judged."*

I therefore urge you to pursue experience as the companion of knowledge. For are we not more than the Internet? Are we not inter-beings, inter-connected in ways which transcend the World Wide Web? Let us not be caught in the spider's proverbial web, which has the potential to keep us trapped in a dark and dim place. For knowledge alone can only deliver conceit and labour, whereas experience produces the communion of love and rest. When we follow sacred texts, what we receive are the views of men who lived in the ancient world. When we follow our feelings, we connect to millions of years of evolution, which has kept us alive.

As people we have always held a special energy, which lives within and among us. This energy is a vested intelligence, which can transform humankind. Today all humankind is on the verge of a great tipping point. When we truly become united in our collective genius, a new age will become a reality in the hearts, minds, and souls of all peoples. Humanity has come to understand the principles of consciousness, but as a whole it has not quite reached the energy necessarry to ignite its fire. Each person has a responsibility to achieve *Gnosis*, and nothing else matters as much. There is no other way out of our global crisis, for nothing else has worked or can work. It is only through the unity of a collective cooperation that humankind can acquire the high degree of energy necessary to reach the entire consciousness of humankind.

May all humanity therefore develop the God given courage of *homo spiritualis*, so all peoples may awaken to the endless spiritual delights that await at the table of Christ consciousness. Through the union of both God and Goddess, may the One reveal to all the path of *Gnosis* that will ignite the energies needed to finally push the noosphere over a tipping point into a unifying field of consciousness. For as we collectively arrive at a large scale group consciousness, we can mindfully work toward a more loving coexistence for all life on Mother Earth, and ultimately find a resting place within the cosmic mind of the One.

THE AEONIC AGE
AND THE KISS OF CONSCIOUSNESS

$\mathcal{T}$he geological time scale is a system of dating that relates geological strata to time, and is used by geologists, paleontologists, and other earth scientists to describe the timing and relationships of events that have occurred during Earth's history. According to science, Earth is 4.5 billion years old. The Cenozoic era began about 66 million years ago. The time frame for the evolution of *Homo sapiens* from their ancestors only began roughly 30,000 years ago. The evidence is therefore clear that humans have been on planet Earth for a very short time.

Humans have been tracking their evolution by observing the night sky for centuries. Our ancestors watched the movements of the heavens to learn from Mother Earth. This helped us to survive and thrive by understanding the natural world.

Ancient cultures discovered that every 2,150 years the sun's position in the heavens shifted, which they marked as a new age, ruled by a different sign of the zodiac. These ages are not acknowledged by the science of astronomy; they are astrological ages, which occur because of the motion of Earth known as the precession of the equinoxes, which, for example, causes the identity of the pole star to change over time. This has to do with a slow angular wobble that the Earth maintains on its axis, which is like a spinning top, as it slows down. This wobble is known as a precession. The amount of time it takes for the precession to go through all twelve signs is roughly 25,765 years. This is also called a "great year" and ancient societies were very aware of it. They therefore referred to each 2,150 year period as an age.

Today we are passing from the Age of Pisces into the Age of Aquarius. Some say we are already on the cusp of change, or that we have already passed the cusp and are beginning a new age. You can decide this for yourself by simply looking at the state of the world. *Homo Sapiens* may have existed for 350,000 years, but their modern brain has only developed in the last 30,000 years in what science calls the Great Leap Forward. Therefore the numbers do not lie. For the last 30,000 years our modern brains have been passing through the ages. We are now ready to transcend the Age of Pisces into the next Age of Aquarius and the birthing of *Homo Spiritus*.

In astronomy an aeon is defined as a billion years. The word *aeon* originally meant life, vital force, or being, generation, or a period of time, though it tended to be translated as age in the sense of ages, forever, timeless, or for eternity. Plato used the word *aeon* to denote the eternal world of ideas, which he conceived was behind the perceived world, as demonstrated in his famous allegory of the cave. Christianity's idea of *eternal life* comes from the word for life, *zoe* and a form of *aeon*, which could mean life in the next aeon, the kingdom of God, or Heaven.

The Piscean Age was marked by organized religion and the material, physical reality of nature. However, the Aquarian Age is marked by a metaphysical understanding of the world. This can be seen as the quantum physics of the Aquarian Age shapes a new world view. This new model is ushering in a new reality, depending on who is observing it. This has been proven over and over again by the double slit experiment which shows that energy changes depending on what, or who, is observing it. This experiment shows that atoms will either act as a wave or a particle, depending on the observer.

Carl Gustav Jung, a proclaimed gnostic, stated the following in his theory of *Continuous Incarnation*: *"Each step towards a Continuous Incarnation is a step towards a higher consciousness and a new potential reality in the material world. The unconscious wants to flow into consciousness in order to reach the light. However, at the same time it thwarts itself because it also wants to remain unconscious. This has become known as the individuation process. It will function unconsciously. But it is man's duty to carry through this process consciously."*

As the Aeonic Age asserts itself, individuals will knowingly offer themselves as incarnating vessels of the Holy Spirit. This will begin individually, but as more and more seekers pursue the path of *Gnosis*, an awakened spirit will come to behold a collective consciousness. The psyche will no longer be influenced by Piscean religious communities, but instead, it will be carried by the Aquarian Age of conscious individuals participating in the universal adoration of the God and Goddess of love.

As we continue to shift away from the old fear based system rooted in bad habits and ignorance, we will envision a new reality for ourselves. This new reality will be based on hope and abundance, rather than fear and poverty.

Nothing can stop the ushering in of the Aquarian Age. However, what can happen is people may choose to remain ignorant and unconscious of its presence, which will only permit the shadow side of humanity to continue its domination. If this happens, humanity will suffer needlessly, but if we choose to wake up, then much human suffering will be avoided, and humanity will be able to exist in cooperation, rather than conflict. Collaborative societies have existed in the past. These societies embraced not only God, but also the Goddess. For the future of humanity to awaken from the grip of the shadow, it must include the loving acknowledgement of the Goddess.

To be awakened by the kiss of consciousness means we must courageously embrace intimacy in our lives and live as authentic peoples. To become authentic, we must know ourselves, and be willing to share what we know with others. In turn, others must share themselves with us, as we unconditionally receive them into our hearts. Then, as a unified people we will be able to share in the abundance of Mother Earth.

This may sound utopian to some. However, the alternative would be catastrophic. We are already witnessing individuals who fear their own shadows and are prepping for conflict and calamity. Conspiracy theories abound and are shaping the minds of the ignorant. The "prepping culture," which has taken root in society, is a diversion tactic, based on fear and cast by the shadow. We need to respond to these fears with the counter practice of loving kindness, which lives within *Gnosis*.

As we look around, we can see much failed intimacy in the world. In its wake we find indifference. This indifference leads to isolation, which then becomes the primary ingredient of failed intimacy. The world is becoming more protectionist, and instead of building bridges, it is building walls. Instead of prioritizing what can save the human race, we prioritize what will damn it. This is why governments are still developing weapons of mass destruction, rather than tools of creative determination.

Plato had the foresight to warn that *"the penalty for refusing to participate in politics is that you end up being governed by your inferiors."* What are we destined to become if we continue to let the ignorant and greedy schemers of society rule the communities and nations of the planet? Once again, let us reflect on the words of Plato: *"Justice in life and conduct of the state is possible only if it first resides in the hearts and souls of the citizens."* I therefore urge all humanity to seek *Gnosis* first, and all other forms of goodness will follow.

Today we are experiencing a frightening political decay. This type of impoverishment can only give momentum to fascist moral corruption. Our world is being traumatized by elitism, and the only way out is to confront the perpetrator of corporate and political abuse. Some countries may be better off than others, but if we do not support those being traumatized, it will only be a matter of time before the abuser is knocking at our door, and crossing our borders. We have an opportunity to become a place of refuge for the victims of this ever growing fascism. We can do this by investing in activities that possess a soul and foster a renewal of the transcendent virtues of human kind. To do otherwise would be to live in denial and participate in erecting new walls of indifference.

When citizens become active, civil society can change peacefully. However, if citizens wait for the proverbial knock on the door, any act of free speech will become viewed as civil disobedience and punished. As citizens of planet Earth, we must act quickly to inspire one another and the world. We must actively participate in the rebirth of a soulful democracy, which can stand up to the kleptocracy of corporate greed, which is now howling within the political corridors of power. As citizens, we have the power to make government act on behalf of its people. However, if we wait, the howling will hunt free speech down and devour it in the streets. The time to act, and the time for *Gnosis*, is now. Through the growth and evolution of *Gnosis*, both individually and collectively, all can be accomplished through non-violence citizen ecumenism.

POIMANDRES

*P*oimandres is an ancient and rare surviving text from Alexandria. It is a prime source of *gnostic* speculation. *Poimen* is Greek for shepherd. It can be translated as the *Mind of the Shepherd* or the *Divine Mind*. In the style of the Socratic method, it proposes a dualistic view of life between the struggle of everything mortal and that of the mind (*nous*). The following is an excerpt from *The Poimandres*.

"What kind of sin do the ignorant commit that they should be deprived of immortality?" I asked. These things Poimandres said. "Now I will tell you what you no longer hear...because the material body has its source in the abhorrent darkness from which came the watery substance of which the body is composed in the sensible world, and from the body death quenches its thirst...Whoever recognizes and knows themselves enters into the good... If you learn you are also made of light and life, you will return to light and life."

I then asked, "But how shall I come to life?" Poimandres said, "Within the dissolution of your material body your image vanishes. The bodily senses return to their own sources, becoming part of the cosmos, and, combined in new ways, do other work. Anger and desire enter thoughtless nature. Then man rises into the harmony, the world of the spheres. In the first zone it leaves behind the force to grow and decrease, in the second the machinations of evil, in the third the guile of lust, in the fourth domineering arrogance, in the fifth unholy daring and rashness, in the sixth striving for wealth by evil means, and in the seventh zone the malicious lie. All rendered powerless.

"Then stripped naked by the force of harmony, enters into the eight sphere of the fixed stars, and possessing their own energy remains there with others singing and are happy…All move in order up to the father and surrender powers, and become powers, and are in God…This is the good, the aim of those who have Gnosis, to become God…Now that you have received everything from the Father, why not make yourself a guide to the worthy so people may be saved by God through you"…and, having said these things, Poimandres before my eyes mingled with the powers.

I thanked and blessed the Father of all, and was sent forth, empowered and instructed concerning the nature of all and with supreme vision. I began to talk to the people of beauty, piety and Gnosis…"O people born of the Earth, given over to drunkenness and sleep and ignorance of God, end your drunkenness and unreasoning sleep…Why have you accepted death when you have been given the power to enjoy immortality?…Change your ways, you who walk in error and keep company with ignorance…Free yourself of darkness and seize the light, abandon corruption and receive immortality"…Some mocked me and left me, for they had given themselves to death. But others were guided by the sowed words of wisdom in them and they were nourished with ambrosial water. When evening came and the rays of the sun began to fade, they thanked God…and when they completed their thanksgiving, each sought his or her own bed.

All this happened to me, since I have received it from my mind, that is, from Poimandres, the word and mind of absolute sovereignty. I became God inspired, God minded, and came with the truth.

True power exists to create positive change in the here and now. There have been many great spiritual leaders over the life span of humanity: Socrates, Buddha, Confucius, Rumi, Mani, and Jesus, just to name a few. Each had a central message for humanity—that the only way people can wake up from the grip of the lower manifestations of the self or ego is to strive to enter into the higher and free associations with wisdom. This wisdom has been called *de, the way, virtue, morality, Gnosis,* etc. Plato's analogy of the cave is a good example of the way humans are seduced and hindered in their pursuit of happiness. In fact, each of the above mentioned spiritual leaders all gave humanity many ways to find happiness within. Herein rests the key to happiness. For it is the ultimate test of each individual person to awaken to whatever distraction is keeping them trapped in the cave of their own choosing. In the end, each of these spiritual geniuses' lives can be distilled into three words: virtue, happiness, and love. This trinity of essence and being is all we have to be concerned with to live the life we have been born to live. Essentially, if we live a virtuous life, we will become happy, and find the love we are searching and have been created for. It is that simple. Each of these men suffered at the hands of inferior personalities, and was sacrificed by spiritually immature authorities.

For these men *Gnosis* brought them to the threshold of death, a death they willingly accepted. However, they knew that the death of the physical body was not the end. This is why we will always have spiritual giants to continue to show us *the way*. They will never stop coming into our lives to introduce us to a new consciousness. In the New Age, the evolving wisdom of Sophia and the Goddess will birth a new *way*. This new *way* is available to everyone right now. But no one can be forced to discover what they defy. Even the Buddha could not force anyone to wake up. It is the task given to each and every one of us freely and individually. However, once experienced, we can bask in this new awareness and share what we have learned. What we can pray for is that the next spiritual leaders who arrive can replace the antiquated religious and political systems of governance which are contributing to the death of Mother Earth. We must pray that as we grow individually and collectively, our religious and political leaders will come to possess a soul that will motivate a stewardship free of greed and corruption.

As we search the planet, can you see the next leader? There are many good people out there, just as there are many evil people out there. But who is the next Buddha, Socrates, Confucius, Rumi, Mani, or Jesus? The answer in the Age of Aquarius is that the next leader is not just one individual.

This is why no matter how hard you look, no one can be found. This is also why the world is waking up to the many charlatans who still exist. For thousands of years the world has been supplied with a steady stream of spiritual guides who have provided mentorship, instruction, and spiritual direction. However, there will be no individual leader in the future. If we keep looking and waiting for one leader, we will be deceived by gurus, corporations and politicians. The new leaders will be *Us, We, The People*. You and me—all of humanity as the evolution of *Homo Spiritus*. In the new Aquarian Age all humanity will possess Buddha consciousness, Confucian consciousness, Socratic consciousness, Rumi Consciousness, Mani consciousness and Jesus consciousness. We will all have the opportunity to be enlivened by the consciousness of the great spiritual leaders, as one divine energy living in all peoples. This one divine energy is what we will call Christ consciousness.

The world is prepared for a new leadership, a new

leadership which can share in a collective mind. The collective mind will produce more than a single spiritual leader. It will produce many leaders within the collective pure saving grace of Christ consciousness.

This is revealed to us in a verse from the *Gospel of Gnosis*: *My hand is on the man I have chosen. First go to the places good men go. Then go to those other places and they will follow.* This is the manna from heaven for the world to consume. This is the *Gnosis* of Christ consciousness.

A NEW RENAISSANCE AND *HOMO SPIRITUS*

$\mathcal{T}$he sun illuminates the surface of the moon; however, the moon still has a dark side. We humans are also illuminated on the surface, but possess a dark side. It is deep within our dark side where the treasure is buried. The more we uncover our shadows through *Gnosis*, the more we can awaken to the cooperative beauty of loving kindness.

Each day, as the world turns, it fluctuates between light and darkness. And as we sit on this rotating planet in the middle of the cosmos, we think we know how our day will unfold. Often we are thrown a curve ball, but somehow we cope. But what happens when we have something thrown at us that we cannot deal with? As humans we have traditionally reacted in different, but predictable ways. For instance, we may become angry, violent, depressed, or we can become creative and inventive. Today we are living in a world where we desperately need more of the latter.

As humans, we are now facing the very real possibility of our own extinction—not by a massive volcanic eruption, or asteroid, which may also be a possibility, but by something much more sinister, called human ignorance, which could cause humans to employ weapons of mass destruction. However, at the time of writing these words, we are being warned by the world's scientists that the more likely reason for the extinction of humanity, and many other forms of life, will be climate change, which in turn could also cause our struggle for survival to trigger a nuclear war. In either case, whether by war or natural disaster brought on by human ignorance, the end result would be the same. We will simply not be able to exist on a planet which is no longer friendly. How is this possible? How have we alienated this most precious of relationships with Mother Earth? Why have we slowly been turning the Garden of Eden into a wasteland? Have we not been warned over and over again to look into our dark side, to find how to make life worth living? Maybe this little play on words can give us the answer. What is meant by the phrase *worth living*? What are we worth? Is wealth the measure of worth, or is worth the measure of wealth? To measure success by the material standard is the genius of the ignorant. This is why there are many intelligent people steering commerce, but poverty still abounds around the world.

Our value systems are all mixed up, turned upside down. In the world we have created, nothing can happen without money or some type of currency to barter with. The next big thing may be Bitcoins. But regardless of whether we barter with sheaves of wheat or Bitcoins, the system is flawed, because it was invented by ignorant, flawed people—the same ignorant, flawed people who are still calling the shots, because they believe in the illusion of a superficial monetary system for measuring worth.

> *Those who lose themselves in their desire for things*
> *also lose their innate nature by being vulgar.*
> *They are known as people who turn things upside down.*
>
> *Chuang Tzu*

Here is a question that will hopefully cut even quicker to the point at hand, which is, how can all life on the planet survive human greed and ignorance? Well, the answer is to wake up to *Gnosis*. But for those asleep this is folly. For example, here is how presbyters of the moral authority can enhance their spiritual sincerity and credibility: why don't institutions, like churches, temples, synagogues, lodges, etc., stop supporting real estate? Let the cathedrals and structures built of brick and mortar become museum pieces dedicated to the past. Let present and future elders of religious movements shun the trappings of organized religion and turn back to nature. Let them stop spending millions building new cathedrals and temples. These physical institutions may have had their purpose in the past, but their time is over. This is evident, as we see attendance at these places of worship shrink. The empty pew is a phenomenon which actually validates the view that humanity is moving toward a major paradigm shift. It is now time to stop worshipping the sacred cow. I guarantee the reaction to such a proposal would be, *ARE YOU CRAZY?* What would abandoning cathedrals and temples accomplish? Well, firstly, they should not be abandoned; they should be preserved as sacred places, just like any historical artifact is preserved in a museum. These standing museums can be monuments to our past, which will document our collective human journey thus far.

What is required for humanity to move forward in such a way is a drastic shift in consciousness. Those already stuck in the illusion of the market place have already been seduced to such an extent that they cannot give up what they have. So to expect those stuck in the past to suddenly become the redeemers of the future is truly what can be called a crazy and unrealistic expectation. This task will have to fall on the youthful and the few who are willing to give up what they have to move forward into a different consciousness—a consciousness which is more evolved and in tune with what is necessary for planet Earth to survive. In a nutshell, those who have little, have very little to give up. They are less attached to the trappings of the world and therefore are open to embracing the new world view of sharing communities. Instead of the 1% controlling the future of humankind, the 99% will determine the future under the mantel of a resource system which is concerned with the fair distribution of wealth.

Gurus, cults and corporations may say this is ludicrous, but it is not. Let me illustrate it this way. If religion was banished, would people all of a sudden become evil? Of course not! On the contrary, they would probably become more compassionate free thinkers. Would people stop caring for the poor all of a sudden? Of course not! Acts of kindness would continue without religion or clergy. By the same rationale, if corporations were abolished, would the world fall apart? Of course not! The stock market might crumble, but that would only be a temporary adjustment, as the world would return to a more natural way of functioning. In the minds of the corporate elite it might feel like the end of the world, but in truth, they would only be giving back that which did not really belong to them in the first place. This reversal of fortune could be interpreted as the process of equalization, dating back to the early aristocracies who, through the guise of imposed royal charters, were able to steal from the peasant class. History has revealed that serfdom ended when artisans formed guilds, and were finally able to make a life for themselves and their families. However, royal charters put an end to the prosperity of guilds and the die was cast when royal charters eventually became the first corporations. So, in reality, not in a distorted corporate reality, the world could function quite nicely and more naturally without corporations. In fact, a more natural world is just what we need.

> *I started with what I knew,*
> *matured my innate nature,*
> *and allowed destiny to do the rest.*

> *Chuang Tzu*

Those who can practice loving detachment will have a less difficult time giving up what they don't really need. Since they will only be giving up an illusion, they will more easily embrace a future, which is not dependent on a monetary resource system founded on greed. What they will embrace is a practical resource-based system devoted to the shared distribution of wealth. For this to happen, the elders and presbyters of the community must take the first steps, so others may have a guiding light to lead them into a new renaissance.

This next renaissance is a necessary step, which will meet with much resistance from the entrenched status quo of the monetary elites. These monetary elites exist in all sectors of society, from church to state. Therefore, we can expect the old violent behavior of a dying monetary system to lash out against this new renaissance. Unless this old vanguard wakes up to *Gnosis*, they will not be able to comprehend that when they strike out against the future, they will also be striking out against themselves.

This new renaissance will be the birthing of the next evolution of humanity. This next evolution of humanity will be known as *Homo Spiritus*, and will not be motivated by greed or an antiquated monetary system. Humans will become motivated by a resource system that is grounded in nature and respect for Mother Earth. In other words, they will not toil for silver, gold or Bitcoins; they will not slave to make others rich. They will not desire trinkets which do nothing, except create the class distinctions which have enslaved humans for most of their collective history. They will stop supporting outdated systems of oppression, and will be willing to let these systems die with dignity. As a result, a stronger and more compassionate *Homo Spiritus* will walk forth and the relationship between Mother Earth and humanity will be rekindled through the mutual embrace of loving kindness for all forms of life.

The sage is the evidence humanity has that *Homo Spiritus* is with us and has been with us for a very long time. *Homo Spiritus* is made of Heaven and Earth, of father and mother, of yin and yang. *Homo Spiritus* possesses a balance with and within nature. Eventually there will come a day of reckoning and awakening, and then we shall know how much of our life we had actually slept through.

I dreamt that I was a butterfly, flitting around and enjoying myself. I had no idea I was Chuang Tzu. Then suddenly I woke up and I was Chuang Tzu again. But I could not tell, had I been Chuang Tzu dreaming I was a butterfly, or a butterfly dreaming I was Chuang Tzu? However, there must be some sort of difference between Chuang Tzu and a butterfly! We call this the transformation of things.

Chuang Tzu

In the new renaissance *Homo Spiritus* is open to all possibilities. They are willing to plunge into the unknown and the endless to find their authentic self, whether it be a person or a butterfly. Sages understand the importance of looking deeply into the mysteries of life. They are always mining for the treasure buried in the shadow of the psyche. This is why they can live simply. They need and desire little and are much closer to happiness than most everyone else. The birthing of *Homo Spiritus* within the main stream is something which will take time. Who knows how long? But it has started and must continue for the common good of all life on Mother Earth. Today one of the most relevant questions we can ask is, do we have enough time left on the doomsday clock for *Homo Spiritus* to save humanity?

We can turn anywhere and constantly hear technical innovators, business analysts, or retail futurists praising how wonderful humans are and how wonderful the future will become in the world of dataism. All their conjectures and speculations are resting on the foundation of yesterday's old business models. These business models are transactional, and conditional, and motivated by the bottom line of greed. They come with strings attached and are high maintenance for Mother Earth.

The futuristic world of *Homo Spiritus* is less programmed and leaves room for the spirit. Its foundation is rooted in a social resource model which is less contractual, less conditional, and is motivated by loving kindness for the common good. There are no strings attached, and it is very low maintenance for Mother Earth.

In the end, the existing system promotes competition and conflict, while *Homo Spiritus* will promote cooperation and harmony. Which kind of a world would you prefer to live in? What type of a world do you want for your children, grandchildren, and descendants? Finally, do you want to be known as the last generation who had a chance to save humanity, but was too idle and shallow to do anything?

If the only ideas we hear come from the technical

innovators, business analysts, or retail futurists, what chance will we have? Even if we listen to traditional religions, as well meaning as they are, what is new in their message? The voices of the sages have always been with us, because their message transcends time and space. But as soon as they are heeded, some tycoon will quantify the message and try to convert it to dollars. This is why we have so many charlatans who still make a handsome profit as predators of the sheeple. This is also why traditional religion has such a vested interest in the old way of doing things; they promote change, but do not want to give up any power and control to achieve it.

We can all do something, and together we can do even more. But you have to show up! You don't have to go to church; you don't have to show up at revivals. But you do have to find like-minded people who care about Mother Earth and are waking up to *Gnosis*. You do have to take responsibility for your own future, and look into your shadow. You do have to stop being victimized by consumerism, capitalism, patriotism, and any other *ism* you can think of.

Let me put it like this. What do you see when a celebrity is driving a car valued at $5,000,000? What do you think when you hear an athlete is being paid $70,000,000 a year to play a game? What do you feel when you are told that the pornography industry is valued at over 100 billion annually? When you are paying $2.75 a gallon to fill your car up at the gas pump, are you happy that the oil industry revenues are in the trillions? Yes, the oil companies will eventually convert to clean energy, but not until they have profited and raped Mother Earth of every ounce of oil still in her womb.

When I answer these questions, what I see, feel and think is that the measure of success is not how expensive your car is. To me a $5,000,000 car is not a sign of success; it is a sign of ignorance and spiritual immaturity. This is why we need to develop our higher senses and seek the evolution of *Homo Spiritus*.

Mother Earth is the giver and sustainer of life. If we are all dependent on oil, who will be her protector and champion? What can we do? Well, once again, the answer is *Gnosis*, and the need to look within, and take an active part in birthing *Homo Spiritus*.

Characteristics of Homo Spiritus

Homo erectus did not just wake up one morning and find that they had changed into *Homo sapiens*. It was an evolutionary process, a process they probably did not even notice. The difference for *Homo sapiens* is that we have developed a consciousness, which has produced a deep self-awareness. This has revealed to us the evolution of a healing process, which can be identified as an awakening *Homo Spiritus*. Now that humanity has become more mindful, we have the power within to accelerate the birthing and evolution of *Homo Spiritus*. This first step in the birthing process is to embrace *Gnosis*.

A man's life is what his thoughts make of it.

Marcus Aurelius

Homo Spiritus may look physically the same as you and I in the beginning. Over time the evolutionary process may change us physically in different and unique ways. But if we all look physically the same in the beginning, how will we be able to recognize a newborn *Homo Spiritus*? There must be something different we can notice. We have all met people we are attracted to; somehow they just seem to have a pleasant glow, or aura about them. I suggest that if you have met a person like this, you have met *Homo Spiritus*. A *Homo Spiritus* will possess a beauty and aura which elludes many *Homo sapiens*. Other people will be attracted to them, while the *Homo Spiritus* may be more inclined to avoid attention. They are free spirits and thinkers who may seem eccentric at first, but have an uncanny way of

1. They may feel different
2. They are attracted to brightness and sunlight
3. They initially feel uncomfortable when exposed to crowds
4. At times they find day to day living meaningless
5. Generally they shun society and tend to be more reclusive
6. They may be emotionally intense and may experience diverse mood swings
7. They may appear to others to dissociate, but are actually very grounded
8. They may lose track of time
9. They may have some difficulty retaining short term memories
10. They are less interested in linear time
11. They have vivid dreams
12. Others consider them different or a little strange
13. They have difficulty finding like-minded people to be social with
14. They are not always politically correct
15. They are not interested in wealth or power
16. They always see the good in other people, to the point of naïvety
17. They can be easily taken advantage of
18. They possess a strong desire to wake up, change, illuminate, and heal others
19. They are positively rebellious, but respectful
20. They are attracted to mystery and other cultures
21. They are drawn to the metaphysical and theosophical
22. They are interested in developing abstract, philosophical

and spiritual realities
23. They have an aversion to technology
24. They are hypersensitive to physical, emotional, mental and spiritual influences
25. They may appear younger than their chronological age
26. They consciously make an effort to share ideas
27. They are cathartic listeners
28. They are drawn to alternative therapies, lifestyles and medicines
29. They have an innate understanding of birth and death cycles
30. They possess strong opinions, ethical, and moral perceptions
31. They have a love for nature
32. They may feel this life is their last reincarnation
33. They have amnesia of a past existence when the spirit joined with the physical body
34. They have a sense of being protected and watched over by a guardian

making the peculiar seem plausible. The following are a few characteristics, which may help you identify *Homo Spiritus*.

The Renaissance
The word *Renaissance* is derived from the French word meaning rebirth. It was a period from the 14th to the 17th century, and is considered the bridge between the Middle Ages and modern history. It started as a cultural movement in Italy in the late Medieval period, and later spread to the rest of Europe. The Renaissance was a time of great beauty and art.

The New Renaissance
The next or new renaissance will be the next step forward, and

the bridge between the modern era and the new millennium of Aquarius. Its focus will be on the humanization of knowledge, which will increase, rather than decrease, the dignity of life on Mother Earth. Since things like money, fame and economic growth are often quite literally de-humanizing, they will become less important. Life will stop being commodified and living virtuously will become the focus of our shared value systems. On the surface this may all seem far-fetched, but if you look deeper, you will find many small pockets of people who are already trying to live by these shared virtues. It is through these grass root organisms that the humanization of knowledge, and the systematic birthing of *Homo Spiritus*, will manifest in the consciousness of humanity. Do not look to the corporate entity for leadership, for they lack the fertility for the child of *Homo Spiritus* to grow. It will become the task of a mature *Homo Spiritus* to permeate the corporate world, and become the inspiration for their transformation. When institutions, churches, and corporations are populated by *Homo Spiritus*, they will become converted into compassionate remedies for positive change.

Suffering is caused by the behavior patterns of one's own mind.

The Buddha

At the age of 29 Siddhartha Gautama left the palace, leaving his possessions and his family behind. He spent six years meditating on the essence, causes, and cures for human suffering. What he eventually realized was that suffering is not caused by ill fortune, social injustice, or divine providence. He discovered that suffering is caused by the behavior patterns of one's own mind. In other words, it is caused by the lack of *Gnosis*. The Buddha was just a human being like you and me. However, he made a concerted effort and prized his evolution—he became an enlightened *Homo Spiritus*. For all we know, he may have evolved beyond *Homo Spiritus*. Tradition tells us that Jesus also evolved beyond *Homo Spiritus*. There was only one Buddha and one Jesus, just like there is only one you and one me. So with a concerted effort we, too, can evolve beyond our wildest dreams. But we have to start where we are right now, and be willing to take the first step into the darkness of our shadow. Just as Jesus spent time in the desert to battle demons, we, too, must battle our own shadows. We have the promise that if we trust the Christ within, we will be illuminated by the treasure we find buried deep within our souls.

Pico della Mirandola was an Italian scholar and philosopher of the Renaissance. He composed the *Oration on the Dignity of Man*. It is a famous discourse written in 1486 and has been described by modern scholars as the *Manifesto of the Renaissance*. It ends with the following call to action:

Let some holy ambition invade our souls, so that, dissatisfied with mediocrity, we shall eagerly desire the highest things and shall toil with all our strength to obtain them, since we may if we wish.

Pico della Mirandola

Michelangelo is credited with stating, *People of accomplishment rarely sit back and let things happen to them. They go out and happen to things.* This could very easily become the credo of *Homo Spiritus*. Everything is now converging; we only need to embrace it. The future is in our hands.

Sustemas Libertas
The most supreme offering *Homo Spiritus* has for civilization is the revelation that all humanity may be liberated by choosing to embrace *Gnosis*! All of us on Mother Earth have to make

a personal decision. Do we choose to be part of a New Renaissance, which will spiritualize the divine solution to the world's problems, or will we continue to support the obsolete systemic burnout of the human race? In other words, do you choose ignorance or *Gnosis*?

We all have within our power the ability to accelerate the birthing of *Homo Spiritus* by practicing the mindfulness principles of an awakened spirit. It is now more than ever within our power to change the course of human affairs. All we have to do is choose life by simply making the choice to ask for *Gnosis*, and by waking up to the countless options that await the future of humankind. The term *Sustemas Libertas* can be translated to mean *community of freedom*. This freedom begins within the mind of the beholder, and expands to include the community or *anima mundi*. For centuries this *anima mundi*, or universal soul, has experienced the pains of labor and is now ready to give birth to *Homo Spiritus*. Once born, *Homo Spiritus* will not be able to return to the womb, and would never dream of doing so. For once the human spirit has truly risen to see the face of the God and the Goddess, retreat is not an option.

Homo Spiritus is the result of *Gnosis*. It is the incarnation of healing and growth. The reason the church and state are burning out is because they are trying to stop the healing process from happening. But you cannot kill an idea which has been given life eternal by an evolved human spirit. The source of this life has been referred to as the One by all religions and remains constant throughout the cosmos. The One has given us the innate ability to change in harmony with the eternal evolution of the mind, which is the true source of life. It is the source of our life's joys and the antithesis of our desolations. To spiritualize, we must answer the interior calling of the soul, which is unique to each and every one of us. As we spiritualize, we will begin to understand all the contrast, confusion, and paradoxes of life. We must answer the call of spiritualization to progress beyond the unknown, and to find our final rest in the mysterious sanctuary of the One. However, first we must commit to embarking on a healing journey, which is unique to each and every one of us. Once we accept this quest, the interior visions of self-discovery will abound, if we are truly open to receiving them beyond the doubt and criticism of emotional defilement. Then, as the cycle of life continues, we will return over and over again to our rightful place in the cosmos and experience liberation. Our soul will lie to rest the weight of the past, and we will come to know ourselves as never before. Our soul will be free to soar to such heights as we have never known; as we continue the journey of self-discovery, we will feel a well-being and connection to one another and Mother Earth that we have never known before.

We shall not cease from exploration, and the end of all our exploring will be to arrive where we started and know the place for the first time.

T. S. Eliot

In the *Book of Chuang Tzu* we are told the story about three men traveling together along the road of life:

If there are three men walking together and one is confused, they will still reach their goal, because confusion is in the minority. But if two of them are confused, they will not arrive, because confusion is in the majority. So nowadays with so much confusion in the world, I can indicate to the people where to go, but they do not follow me. Distressing, isn't it?

Chuang Tzu

The writer then elucidates the story and states that for a noble person to grow in maturity, they must possess the stability of virtue. In this way a noble person will be magnanimous in their ventures for the benefit of all life. The noble person's actions are described as follows:

> *Such a person will leave the gold in the mountain*
> *and the pearls to lie in the deep.*
> *They do not view money and goods as true profits,*
> *nor are they attracted by fame and fortune,*
> *nor by enjoyment of long life,*
> *nor sadness at an early death,*
> *they do not value wealth as a blessing,*
> *nor be ashamed of poverty.*
> *They will not lust for the wealth of a generation to have as their own.*
> *They have no wish to rule the whole world as their private domain.*
> *Their honor is clarity of understanding*
> *that all life is part of one treasury,*
> *and that death and birth are united.*
> *Their knowledge is firmly rooted in the origin of self*
> *and encompasses even the spirits.*
> *Their heart goes out to what is beyond them.*
> *Without virtue their body has no brightness.*
> *They move unexpectedly and all life comes after them.*

To some this may sound ludicrous. But I can assure you, if humanity would only give themselves an opportunity to truly avoid the world of distraction, a new paradigm could begin to unfold within their minds and hearts. Patterns exist in the heavens for those who dare to look up from their keypads. It is said that we become like the thing we love. So we must learn to choose wisely. Fish can live in water contentedly. But if people were to try to live in water, they would die. Different people need

different things to live. We all must find the right environment
to flourish. To do so, we must wake up to the truth that living
in a submarine is not the same as living under water. This is
simply living in a metal tube, which is filled with air and sinks
to the bottom of the pool. Likewise, people cannot fly. Birds
can fly, but people cannot. Being propelled through the air,
sitting in a metal tube above the clouds, is not flying; it is simply
being corralled in a metal tube, which is being hurled across
the sky. To think otherwise is just another illusion. Therefore,
we must learn to let a fish be a fish and a bird be a bird; we
must let them have what the Creator has given them. Likewise,
humans must respect and celebrate what the Creator has given
to us. A bird does not want to be a human, so why should we
want to be a bird? When we stray from our natural path, all we
do is upset the balance of nature. As we trace human history,
the only achievement accomplished by this type of mentality
has been the extinction of millions of species. It is time to stop
upsetting the balance of nature; it is time to use our human gifts
to repair the damage we have inflicted on Mother Earth. It is
time to admit to the birds that we cannot fly; it is time to admit
to the fish that we cannot live in the sea. And finally, it is time
to admit to Mother Earth that we have abused her. In doing so,
may all life on Mother Earth show us mercy and forgiveness. As
humanity steps into tomorrow, may *Homo Spiritus* sincerely show
contrition by seeking to live in balance and harmony within the
entire realm of biodiversity. In doing so, may once again
become a respected companion and friend of the natural world.

If a footpath in the mountains suddenly begets a lot of use, it becomes a
road. And if it never gets used, it is soon choked with underbrush. In this
way the wise and worthy used their bright insight to open bright insight in
people. Today authorities use blind ignorance and attempt to open bright

insight in people.

Mencius

ELEMENTAL HEALING

*T*he *therapeutica* is the healing nature of *Gnosis*. Those who choose to embrace the healing principles of the *therapeutica* innately express their desire to love and be loved. In doing so, they are making a conscious decision to advance *Homo Spiritus* in their lives. As a result, they are also contributing to the mutual advancement of humanity and the common good.

The problems that exist in the material world can only be solved by a concerted effort by the patrons of *Gnosis*. Change does not happen from the top down; it comes from the grass roots. Therefore, we will not be able to find a political or secular solution to spiritual problems. As *Gnosis* awakens humanity, *Homo Spiritus* will naturally be destined to create a gathering place for a *therapeutica* to come together as one. This gathering will not necessarily be tangible; it will have no central leadership, and will therefore be invisible to the unkind who wish it to be destroyed. It will flourish under the great protector of love.

The future of humanity depends on its ability to heal. In many instances, a lot of healing is a reaction to ignorance. As a result, individuals need to learn how to stop reacting to ignorance. In other words, we are so accustomed to living in a dysfunctional state of being, we perceive this state to be natural, when it is really unnatural. Unnatural healing exists because humanity has been conditioned to react to the symptoms of ignorance, and not its cause. The alternative to this dysfunction is to learn how to respond to symptoms of ignorance by responding to its causal factors. Once humanity addresses the cause of ignorance, we will begin to heal personally and generationally. The need for generational healing is a very important reality to comprehend, as humanity is increasingly being seduced by a monetary based western medical model. This model supports a high tolerance for sickness, martyrdom, and all kinds of inappropriate coping mechanisms. It is so entrenched in our western medical model, that it is almost impossible to find anyone to publicly speak out against it. This is the power of greed.

The current medical model is what we have been prescribed to numb the senses. But there is another model, called the behavioral model. Let us now use it to look at the future of healing. This model can be illustrated by comparing the body to a motor vehicle. When driving a car, you should spend most of your time looking ahead, and not staring into the rear view mirror. A rear view mirror should only be used occasionally to see what you are leaving behind. Looking forward is the only way to drive down the road of life.

The reason people fail to discover their authentic self is because they are trapped in the past. They fail not because of what they know about the past, but because of what they fail to accept about the future. They might know what needs to be done, but they fail to do it. As a result, people fail to take the road less travelled.

For instance, an alcoholic may very well know they must stop drinking in order for their life to reap the peace and contentment of sobriety. But they fail to believe in themselves and the future. As a result, they are stuck in the energies of the past and are trapped repeating the same energy cycles over and over again. They may sincerely want to stop drinking, and plan to do so tomorrow, but for the alcoholic tomorrow never comes. In their intellect they cannot transcend the past and present, and project into the future. They constantly repeat unhealthy cycles, because they fail to attempt anything in the future which could bring them relief and healing. Of course, no one can explain this to them. This is the truth of direct experience. Whether it is a manifestation of pain or joy, your experience is your own, and any direct energy you experience is also your own, until you decide to share it. To share your truth is an intimate challenge and is a stumbling block for many. Failed intimacy due to a lack of emotional intelligence is a scourge of our modern times.

Personal transformation and wellness do not result from living in our past—the past is an anchor to our dysfunction. True healing is a gift from the future. Remember, there is nothing new to create; there are only endless configurations of energy waiting to be discovered. These endless fields of energy have always existed, so they cannot be destroyed, or re-created. The Creator has already done this for us. Our task as humans is to discover them for ourselves and embrace them in the purest form. This type of healing is what will help *Homo Spiritus* to evolve. *Homo Spiritus* has been called to continue along the path of evolution. On this path they will discover the integrative energy concepts of quantum healing. Quantum energy healing focuses on giving the body back its energy balance in order to facilitate healing, without having to resort to medical interventions, such as surgery, or medications. The main idea behind quantum energy healing is that the human body has the natural ability to heal itself. Every person has a different experience with quantum healing and a different relationship with his or her own body, mind, and soul.

Quantum healing is difficult to explain. Scientists attempt to explain it through the discipline of quantum physics. However, most of us do not understand the principles behind quantum physics. And in all honesty, scientists are the first to admit that they do not understand it either. But as scientists become the more enlightened high priestesses and priests of tomorrow, they will do their best to capture the essence of quantum physics in a language we can all come to understand. For this is the quest God has laid before humanity: to search for the Creator's essence. As we continue the search, we will continue to grow, evolve, and heal as *Homo Spiritus*.

A state of spiritual, mental, and physical wellness will enable *Homo Spiritus* to lead an active, meaningful, and fulfilling life, and realize her or his higher full potential. The goal they set for their life is to achieve abiding spiritual enlightenment, happiness, and peace. An individual at peace with oneself is like a river flowing into the sea. They can influence all of humanity. Spiritual awareness gives *Homo Spiritus* the light of wisdom, and a sense of spiritual confidence. Thus, the path they have chosen will lead to a meaningful and fulfilling life. This is the inner light, which casts no shadow, and lights the path ahead in all directions.

Homo Spiritus will blaze a new path of discovery. In their quest for truth they will uncover a new sacred book buried deep within the human psyche. This book is written in a code which each and every one of us must decipher for ourselves; it has been written in our DNA by the hand of God. This is the true sacred book which we are called to follow. This book will not incite war and division; it will give rise to peace and harmony. As humans, we share in the Creator's DNA, and therefore have the same narrative written on our common souls. This narrative written by God is indeed the sacred text which has been given to us to aid in discovering the answers to the age-old questions of who we are and what gives life purpose and meaning. Humanity will come to know that the only place to find the answers to life's deepest questions and desires can only be found within the heart and soul of the pilgrim—*Homo Spiritus*. All humanity has to do is dare to open this sacred book, which has been written by the Creator, and is buried deep in our souls, waiting to be discovered.

Most of us cannot explain how our current electronic inventions, like cell phones and computers, work. We may have a rudimentary understanding of energy fields, but this is not enough to adequately explain how theses gadgets truly work. However, this does not stop us from benefitting from their use. Likewise, *Homo Spiritus* has learned how to embrace the future by accepting the gifts of quantum healing. They may not necessarily know how to explain how it works, but this does not stop them from benefitting from its use. As *Homo Spiritus* continues to evolve, they will embrace the new matrix of quantum healing. This matrix is where humanity will discover a new Garden of Paradise. As *Homo Spiritus* walks the Earth, they will become the vessel which will receive all the spiritual delights which the future has to offer. For instance, we already know that contemplation and meditation have the potential to change our elemental make up—it can produce such changes as to deliver us to greater happiness, insight, and wakefulness. Through quantum healing wakefulness can be transformed into blissfulness. Becoming mindful of our own potential and abilities is the healing which the soul is searching for. Through this healing our true purpose can be discovered, and when we discover our true purpose, we will see the true face of the One staring back at us. Then we will know beyond any shadow of a doubt what we must do next. As the view from the mountain top is owned, we will be stripped away of all that is not of God. Then humanity will be ready to follow the light, which will leave us wanting more. This desire will allow us to continue our journey to ascend the next mountain.

I would hypothesize that quantum healing has been with us since the beginning of time. I would further theorize that everyone, from our oldest ancestors to the present, have been unwittingly guided by the spiritual realities of quantum healing. It is only now, under the mantel of *Homo Spiritus*, that we are beginning to identify the sacredness of an old and almost forgotten *therapeutica*.

There has been much written on the subject of quantum healing, so it is not necessary to delve here into its inner working. For in truth, I have not been given the gift of intellectual prowess. But what I have been given, is my own personal experience, which has no dependency on faith. If I possess *Gnosis*, then like operating a simple cell phone or computer, all I really need to know is how to turn it on to receive the information I need. Who really understands how *Gnosis* works? No one! But I am grateful that it exists. For gratitude is the virtue which comprehends that no life ever toils in vain. At the end of our days we can be secure in knowing that all life is but an individual thought of the One. *Homo Spiritus* only needs to discern the information it receives from *Gnosis*. In this way, the spiritual quest will metaphorically bring *Homo Spiritus* to the mountain top of quietude, to reveal a space for a still inner voice to be heard. In this moment we will know that our essence is resilient and can only rest in the presence of the One Great Spirit of Love!

If I speak in the tongues of men or angels, but do not have love, I am only a resounding gong or a clanging cymbal. If I have the gift of prophecy, and can fathom all mysteries and all knowledge, and if I have a faith that can move mountains, but do not have love, I am nothing. If I give all I possess to the poor, and give over my body to hardship, that I may boast about, but do not have love, I gain nothing.

Love is patient, love is kind. It does not envy, it does not boast, it is not proud. It does not dishonor others, it is not self-seeking, it is not easily angered, it keeps no record of wrongs. Love does not delight in evil, but rejoices with the truth. It always protects, always trusts, always hopes, always perseveres.

Love never fails. But where there are prophecies, they will cease; where there are tongues, they will be stilled; where there is knowledge, it will pass away. For we know in part and we prophesy in part, but when completeness comes, what is in part, disappears. When I was a child, I talked like a child, I thought like a child, I reasoned like a child. When I became an adult, I put the ways of childhood behind me. For now we see only a reflection, as in a mirror; then we shall see face to face. Now I know in part; then I shall know fully, even as I am fully known.

And now these three remain: faith, hope and love.
But the greatest of these is love.

1 Corinthians

THE KNOTS OF VIRTUE

*W*e are but guests in this world. Therefore, to progress in the light of virtue, we must learn to take on difficulties, while they are still small and easy to measure. Beware of people who offer a quick and easy way, for their path brings many difficulties. The practice of living virtuously only becomes difficult when we let the little things grow to block the flow of virtuous energies. The more virtue becomes blocked, the more we may feel all tied up. When one knot begets another, it is more difficult to untie them. We can see our lives as a metaphorical big ball of string tied up in copious knots. Just thinking about unraveling this ball of knots may be overwhelming, but once we learn to live in the present, we can unravel one knot at a time.

This is what *Gnosis* can do for us. It is not secret knowledge, though the world would have us believe that it is. It is a wisdom which is available to each and every one of us through direct experience of the One. All we have to do is possess the will to look for it. The first question we must answer is, Am I ready to look for *Gnosis?* The next question will logically be, Where will I look? The answer to both of these questions is the same: look within. We must look at ourselves.

We must turn to the therapeutic community within our collective consciousness; then the church of the mind can become the true temple of the Holy Spirit, and the grace of personal healing. Once we realize that all answers are within us, then the One will become part of our lives and the dependency on gurus will end. Once we discover our inner sage, we will also find others who have embarked on the same journey from their own perspective. As we unravel our balls of knots, we will meet others who can help us along our personal path of discovery. By the same token, we will also become helpful to others, as they progress on their journey of healing. There are many simple examples of this type of peer support available to us. Take a close look at any 12-Step Program. However, those searching to ignite *Homo Spiritus* will surpass the limits of any human construct of the mind.

Today the world is saturated with religious and political systems, which are fueled more and more by frustration, anger, and violence. When the right demigod appears at the right time, who knows what will be born. This is why dogma and theology must always come second to the healing arts. The therapeutic process is paramount for the evolution and growth of consciousness. It is only through a healthy consciousness that any direct democracy or participatory social system can become a true and worthy mechanism for change.

Let us return to the time of the Magi, as it was experienced by the *Therapeutae*. The meaning of the name *Therapeutae* is *healers*. The *Therapeutae* were an ancient order of mystical ascetics who lived in many parts of the ancient world, but were found especially near Alexandria, the capital city of ancient Egypt. This pre-Christian group of ascetics is known today from the writings of Philo of Alexandria, who described the group in his *De Vita Contemplativa* (*On the Contemplative Life*), written around 10

C.E. Philo compared the *Therapeutae* to the Essenes, as both sects were known for their exemplary religious devotion and ascetic practices. According to Philo, communities of *Therapeutae* were widely established in the ancient world, but the particular sect near Lake Mareotis, south of Alexandria in Egypt, was quite famous for its healing arts. The *Therapeutae* were renowned for both their asceticism and healing abilities. Indeed, the English words *therapy* and *therapeutic* are etymologically connected to the name of this ancient spiritual order, indicating that medicine, religion, and healing were deeply connected in the ancient world. In fact, healing was seen as a religious art.

The *Therapeutae* were forerunners of and the model for the Christian practice of an ascetic life. The practices described by Philo were considered as one of the first models of Christian monastic life. Eusebius of Caesaerea, the historian of Christianity, was so sure of the identification of *Therapeutae* with the earliest Christians, that he deduced that Philo, who admired them so, must have been a Christian himself.

We must also acknowledge and respect that as the *Therapeutae* were active in one part of the world, natural healing was also occurring in cultures everywhere on Mother Earth. For example, in a part of the world which became known as the Americas, the same process of healing existed. Today the *Therapeutae* is just a history lesson for many cultures, while the shamanic culture of the Americas is still present and relevant. The growth and spread of the healing energies of the shaman is a gift to all of us and must be recognized by main stream religion. As the Orthodox Church loses its relevance in contemporary society, as evidenced by the empty pew, the rise of shamanic and shamanka culture is now once again taking its rightful place. Now that years of oppression and attempts to systematically exterminate shamanka and shamanic cultures have failed, aboriginal, First Nation, Inuit and Metis spirituality is once again offering a way back to *Gnosis* and harmony with Mother Earth.

Having barely survived genocide, the oral traditions of native peoples across the planet have now become our saving grace. Just as the early Europeans were saved from extinction by starvation in the wilderness of Turtle Island by its native peoples centuries ago, today's aboriginal peoples are once again prepared to turn the other cheek by embodying the Christian virtue of forgiveness towards their oppressors.

The evidence that we must return to the healing arts is obvious, as technologies continue to grow, because they are not reducing the pain and suffering in the world—not because they cannot, but because people lack the will, and do not have proper political leaders who can consolidate a creative solidarity among the peoples of Mother Earth. We must remember that technologies are inanimate, and when manipulated by greed, they can become a destructive force, just as easily as they can become a constructive force, when motivated by enlightened generosity.

The role of the individual, cleric, priest, priestess, elder, tau, shaman, or shamanka, is to grow personally and spiritually, and then share what they know with others. Then they can become a means for the companion seeker to grow personally and spiritually. We don't need to make a better computer; we only need to make a better self. Then maybe the children of Mother Earth will have a better chance at solidarity. This solidarity can only come to pass by embracing *Gnosis*. As we grow in *Gnosis*, we will pass through higher and higher levels until we reach full awareness and enlightenment. I believe we have all been born with an intrinsic desire to achieve full consciousness. So what is stopping us?

In doing so we must remember the words of *Luke 2:52* describing how Jesus sat with the elders in the temple:

> *...and he went down with them and came to Nazareth, and he continued in subjection to them, and his mother treasured all these things in her heart. And Jesus kept increasing in wisdom and stature, and in favor with God and men.*

Just as Jesus had to grow in awareness and consciousness, so must we all grow personally and spiritually! Then, after our time in the desert, we, too, will discern our life's purpose. Therefore, the role of *Homo Spiritus* is to bring humanity to the next level of self-awareness and healing. If religion wants to remain relevant, it can no longer be about dogma, rules, and regulations. It must now embrace healing and offer itself as a sacred space for all peoples to heal. Likewise, if corporations want to remain relevant, they, too, must embrace healing. If they do not, then they will have to prepare for a future of preppers and anarchy. However, the longer they resist healing, the more irrelevant they will become. The only thing that can save secularism and religion is an awakened humanity, led by an enlightened *Homo Spititus*. We do not need to reinvent the wheel, unless we break it completely. In this case, Mother Earth will give us what we ask for through climate change. However, if we choose to restructure corporate board rooms under the guidance of *Homo Spiritus*, then humankind can discover fire for the second time in history. Only this time, the great fire will burn within the hearts, minds, and spirits of an evolved *Homo Spiritus*.

A still mind can easily hold the truth.
The difficulties yet to come can be easily avoided.
The sage desires that which has no desires,
and teaches that which cannot be taught.
They rest in tranquility,
and do not value the objects held by a few,
but only that which is held by everyone.
They guide the seeker back to their own treasure,
and help all things come to know the truth they have forgotten.

Tao Te Ching

Much of what humanity espouses to be spiritual is antidotal. There is no proof that this type of revelation is from the One. This is not to say that this type of direct experience is not valid; in fact, it is an important part of our spiritual journey. However, it is only the beginning. Antidotal experiences cannot be taken as gospel, nor can they be ignored. What we need to do with these experiences is properly discern them. We must determine where an experience is directing us. There is much to learn along the path of *Gnosis*, which must be clearly understood.

Beware of those who come to devour in my name. Always put goodness as well as evil to the trial as a test for the Holy Spirit. For the resurrection is here now and always. Remember, those who are only beginning will think differently about these things.

Gospel of Gnosis, 10.2-3

True *Gnosis* may seem merely antidotal on the surface. This is why we must look deep into its meaning. Like the layers of an onion, we must peel back its surface to uncover deeper and deeper purpose and meaning. This is why in our interior life we must honor our spirit guides. Spirit guides can protect us and bring into the light both truthful and false interior movements of the soul. For instance, here are some simple guidelines to discern the difference between the holy and unholy; there are many others to choose from. One common principle to keep in mind when doing so is to remember that anything which attempts to take away your freedom in any way, shape, or form should be avoided. For the Creator seeks to liberate and foster a free thinking spirit which is confident and willing to challenge both the God and Goddess within all sentient life.

1. In the beginning souls are easily tempted, because they are steeped in ignorance. This ignorance is supported by the lower self, which is easily distracted.
2. An easily distracted soul will fall prey to false consolations.
3. Once false consolations are resisted, desolations, such as shame, guilt, and fear become more apparent.
4. Discern the source for intention, for over time intention may be altered.
5. Good intentions bring consolations that direct interior movements towards the good.
6. Bad intentions direct false consolations away from the good.
7. False consolations cause beguilement.
8. Pure consolations cause joy and peace. Even in the case of pure consolations, the beginning, middle, and end of any interior movement must be discerned.
9. The One will never cause desolation, but may permit it to happen, due to free will and choice. However, the One can always convert a false consolation or false desolation into a real consolation.
10. A real consolation can never be turned into a false consolation or desolation by evil. However, evil may attach

itself to an interior movement with the hope of influencing it at some time in the future.

11. All desolation has at its root ignorance of the Divine Self within.

12. At times, spiritual growth may seem dry, but this should not be confused with desolation.

13. When dryness occurs, the lower self of ignorance may try to convince the higher self to abandon the work of the soul. This is another form of beguilement.

14. Interior emotions are not meant to hurt us; they are meant to guide us to perfection. Therefore, emotional defilement is to be understood as another form of beguilement.

15. Rituals and habits are not part of our true self. Rituals and habits may instill unconscious trance behavior or conscious mindfulness. Therefore, like with everything else, we must discern the intellectual visions which rituals and habits admit into our professions of faith.

16. The practice of mindfulness and the examination of daily encounters should be discerned within the daily cycles of birth, death, and resurrection.

The human narrative is both luminous and nebulous in nature. It is luminous in its ability to guide us into a deeper awareness of who we are. The nebulous keeps alive the mysteries of life, which will always be waiting to lead *Homo Spiritus* safely through the *Way of Gnosis*. As *Homo Spiritus* awakens, they will mature beyond simple antidotal insight. As this evolution unfolds, the unknowable mysteries of life will unfold as part of a new conscious awareness. This new awareness will no longer be indebted to a simple faith, which has been susceptible to abuse for far too long. Acts of faith will become acts of knowledge, based on a more formidable comprehension of the One. The *Way* will become clearer and the road we follow will become knowable. As the mysteries of the unconscious become knowable, *Homo Spiritus* will be offered the divine clarity of *Gnosis* to rescue humanity from their self-imposed bondage of ignorance.

> Jesus said, *Those who seek should not stop seeking until they find. When they find, they will be disturbed. When they are disturbed, they will marvel, and will rule over all.*

> *Gospel of Thomas*

To save ourselves and arrive at this place of *Gnosis*, we only need to do one thing—look within. Then follow the healing graces which can free humanity from a millenium of generational pain and suffering. Then love will be spread across the planet and the arms of Mother Earth will embrace us across the cosmos.

> *Ask and it will be given to you, seek and you will find, knock and the door will be opened to you.*

> *Matthew 7:7*

Humanity has now come to a great evolutionary tipping point. We have come to a point when we all possess the ability to call forth *Homo Spiritus* within. All we have to do is ask. Those who ask will develop the mindfulness to see beyond the precipice; those who refuse to embrace the future of humanity will be at risk of falling into a great abyss. Let us now choose *Gnosis* and make a conscious decision to return to the religious arts of an enlightened contemporary *therapeutica*. May we individually and collectively seek the healing of the human race, so we can once and for all eternity return to our rightful place within the Gardens of Paradise.

A PRAYER FOR CHRIST CONSCIOUSNESS

Bless this sacred union of spirit and soul.

Give us purpose, strength and faith.

Fill our hearts with the joy and wonder that is you.

Remind us moment by moment of your promise

That we hold a place between us.

And as we humbly call forth your presence within us,

Join us forever in what is pure and beautiful in your grace.

Renew us in love.

And through your grace

May we awaken to *Gnosis*.

For in your hands we are one.

In the beginning, God created…
In the end, what will I create?